THE

WRITING GROUP

BOOK

CREATING AND SUSTAINING A SUCCESSFUL WRITING GROUP

EDITED BY
LISA ROSENTHAL

CHICAGO REVIEW PRESS

LIBRARY OF CONGRESS CATALOGING-IN-PUBLICATION DATA

Rosenthal, Lisa.

  The writing group book : creating and sustaining a successful writing group : screenwriters, novelists, playwrights, poets, essayists, memoirists, children's authors / edited by Lisa Rosenthal.— 1st ed.

    p. cm.

 Includes bibliographical references and index.

 ISBN 1-55652-498-6

 1. Authorship—Collaboration. I. Rosenthal, Lisa, 1962– II. Title.

PN145.W756 2003

808'.02—dc21

2003003522

Visit the editor's Web site at **www.lisarosenthal.com** for information on this and other projects.

Jennie Dunham holds the exclusive right to license the republication of her essay "An Agent Among Us: Literary Agents and Writing Groups." Contact: www.dunhamlit.com.

Susan Reuling Furness retains the right to use "Climbing Out of the Snake Pit: A Writing Group Clears a Path to Healing" or an altered version of this work.

Address all correspondence regarding this book to The Writing Group Book Editor in care of Chicago Review Press, or by e-mail at WGB@ipgbook.com.

Cover design and photo: Rachel McClain
Interior design: Monica Baziuk

©2003 by Lisa Rosenthal
All rights reserved
First edition
Published by Chicago Review Press, Incorporated
814 North Franklin Street
Chicago, Illinois 60610
ISBN 1-55652-498-6
Printed in the United States of America
5 4 3 2 1

To the members of my writing group, The Playwrights
Collective, who have helped me grow as an artist
—and—
To Ted, who helps me remember to keep my heart and
mind on the journey and to enjoy the ride

The true brotherhood is not that of the blood,
it's that of sharing.
—RWANDAN PROVERB

[Contents]

PART II

Organizing and Maintaining a Writing Group 55

PART IV

Venturing Beyond the Writing Group Setting 161

Resources

Indexes

[Acknowledgments]

I'D FIRST LIKE to thank playwright Jeffrey Sweet who wrote a wonderful book titled *The Dramatist's Toolkit* and who generously listed his e-mail address on the copyright page. When I wrote to him for advice about my then-dying playwriting group, he gave me some suggestions that revived the group. A special thanks also to Robert Koon who drafted the letter that resparked everyone's interest in our writing group and attracted a new member or two.

I'd like to thank the phenomenal writers in The Playwrights Collective (TPC) who have helped make my writing group such a vital and dynamic experience for me: Vincent Bruckert, Cornelius Collins, Robert Koon, Aline Lathrop, Margaret Lewis, Mia McCullough, Jennifer Miller, Dan Noonan, and Mark Young. Thanks to Claire Geall, Dylan Rice, and Marta Juaniza from the Department of Cultural Affairs, Chicago, who help TPC share its new work with the world.

I'd like to thank the following people who let me pick their brains and glean their wisdom: Gerilee Hundt, Kathy Mirkin, and Linda Matthews. Thanks to Jerome Pohlen who helped me brainstorm some dos and don'ts in the publishing biz, to Allison for helping to keep it all together, to Monica for making it all look so good, and to Rachel McClain for giving the book a great cover. And a special thanks to Cynthia Sherry for believing in this project.

Thanks to all the writers who submitted essays. It was wonderful to discover that there are so many writing groups out there that help sustain, fortify, encourage, and support writers.

I'd like to thank the following people who gave me ideas for the tips lists: E. A. Bagby; Peggy Bird, Ginny Foster, and Jane Mozena; Lisa Dillman; Evan Guilford-Blake; Birdie Stallman Gurvitz; Rasma Haidri; Charlotte Jones; Lila M. Stromer; and Nancy Viau. Whether you were the source for a tip that did or didn't make it through the final editing process, know that I found your words and ideas truly inspirational.

A special note of gratitude to my husband, Ted Hogarth, who not only helps me find the perspective and laughs I desperately need, but also gifts our world with his musical voice and vision, and for playing the meanest baritone saxophone in the world.

Thanks to Anne Lamott, author of *Bird by Bird: Some Instructions on Writing and Life*, who helped light my writing path and shares with all writers droppings of wisdom such as this choice morsel:

> To be engrossed by something outside ourselves is a powerful antidote for the rational mind, the mind that so frequently has its head up its own ass—seeing things in such a narrow and darkly narcissistic way that it presents a colo-rectal theology, offering hope to no one.

And to all those who write or aspire to, thank you for adding this book to your journey of discovery!

Introduction

> **Nothing is more useful to mankind than those arts which have no utility.**
> —OVID

SEVEN YEARS AGO I found myself in a basement classroom of a local playwrights' organization paying more than two hundred dollars to sit around a table, read other participants' plays, and critique them. And I thought, "This is crazy!" I write, I know others who write, and there are people in this class who are very talented writers, so why aren't we forming our own critique group and spending that two hundred bucks on copying scripts, zip disks, and postage? And that's how my playwriting group began. What started as an unnamed, unorganized group of people grew into The Playwrights Collective (TPC). What started as a group of relatively green playwrights in search of a safe haven to try out new work and gain constructive critiques blossomed into a nationally produced and award-winning group of writers. Our once-a-month critique group now meets two or three times each month, shares theater and contest information and marketing tips, attends theater together, and produces a free monthly new play reading series for the people of

Chicago. We also produce an annual festival of new plays that offers local theaters a way to shop for new work, creates new alliances within the theater community, introduces new audiences to the theater, and further enhances the profile of each group member. What did it all cost? Dedication, motivation, and five bucks a year to start the coffee and tea fund.

It does take more than a great idea to create an enduring writing group. But it doesn't need to be complicated. The first step—and I thank the wonderful playwright Jeffrey Sweet for this idea—is regularity. Meeting at a specified time and place creates deadlines and a community that members can count on, and as the familiarity with each other's voice grows, the helpfulness of the feedback increases, and members become more invested in each other's work.

> It is one of the best-kept secrets of fine writers everywhere that if you are lucky, if you are respectful and open, spirit speaks through and to the writer in many ways. This revelation ought not be held away from young writers and new writers especially, for they often feel like fools thinking that only *they alone* hear 'voices.'
> —CLARISSA PINKOLA ESTÉS, author of *Women Who Run With the Wolves*

The Writing Group Book will take you through all the stages of creating and sustaining a productive writing group. Whether you write plays, novels, short stories, children's books, fiction or nonfiction, screenplays, poetry, or choose to write your way through a tragedy, a writing group can provide a safe haven for creative growth as an artist.

The essays in this collection are organized as follows:

- **Part I** includes essays on how to start a writing group whether in person or on-line. Here you'll find essays from writers practicing in diverse genres and from all experience levels.

- **Part II** offers helpful essays on how to organize and maintain a writing group that is fruitful to members and will endure despite conflicts, varying degrees of growth and success, and other challenges. The art of constructive critique is also taught.

- **Part III** features essays on what makes a writing group flourish instead of fizzle or worse, live on as an ineffective entity that chains members to meetings where little creative growth is possible.

- **Part IV** will give you ideas for growing your group in new directions and moving beyond the safe confines of the group itself and into the larger world.

> **The ability to fantasize is the ability to survive.**
> —RAY BRADBURY, novelist

I am grateful for the quality and quantity of essays I received for this collection. The good news is that writing groups are alive and well and growing in popularity. This is not, however, to ignore amazing groups such as the Kansas City Writers Group (see Part III), which will be celebrating its fortieth anniversary shortly.

Ultimately I made some tough choices about which essays to include. The tiebreaker for selecting essays was always whether a particular essay would be helpful to other writers. I have included essays that represent the breadth of issues facing writers today, from how to manage effective critiques, to creating your own writing group when available groups are sub-par, to expanding the range of writing group activities such as writing a group novel, holding a retreat, or creating thematic anthologies.

But just as Katharine Hepburn said, "If you obey all the rules, you miss all the fun," so, too, I've included essays that went beyond my initial selection criteria. For example, Jennie Dunham is a literary agent who submitted a wonderfully informative essay (see Part I) that explains why, with the changing publishing market, writing groups are essential for writers to develop and polish their manuscripts *before* submitting them for agent consideration—the gatekeepers for larger publishing houses—or directly to smaller publishers. Susan Reuling Furness, a writing and poetry therapist, provided an essay (Part II) about finding your voice in journaling groups by combining creativity with self-awareness. I found this essay incredibly inspiring in light of our changing world; I believe it will be inspirational for anyone—writers and nonwriters—struggling to make sense of our changing times. This essay is a great example of how we can cope, process, and find or create a community. It's a testament to the healing power of writing. And my final indulgence was made on behalf of R. Neube because he wrote two exceptionally informative, funny, and unique essays (Part IV) about publishing an anthology of work and then getting rid of—excuse me—*selling* the completed collection to the public. I simply could not choose one over the other without affecting the richness of this collection. Also worth mentioning here are the essays by Karen Lewis (Part II) and Jennifer Tappenden (Part IV), both members of the DCW (only group members know the acronym's meaning) because they exemplify the sharing that happens in writing groups: someone learned of this anthology and shared the information with other members of the group and they *both* submitted wonderful contributions that I am proud to have in this collection. And Deepa Kandaswamy and her on-line group (Part II) is a great example of the universality of the desire to write, connect with others, and communicate with the larger world. Her group includes writers from India, Australia, Ireland, the United Kingdom, Hong Kong, Canada, and the United States.

> **Writing and reading is to me synonymous with existing.**
> —GERTRUDE STEIN

You'll find a variety of writing genres represented in each part of this book and a number of essays from outside the United States including Spain, Norway, India, Israel, and France. Many essays conclude with a list of resources that inspire the essay writer—helpful technical and craft books, useful Web sites, bookstores that are happy assets, inspiring seminars and conferences, and more. Some contributors also provide favorite writing exercises. In the back of the book you'll find lists of more helpful tips to organize a writing group, produce your work, and market it. There are indexes by key word and by type of writing group. Finally, you'll find an invitation and contact information in the event that you or other writing group members would like to submit essays for future editions of *The Writing Group Book*.

In *The Writing Group Book* you'll find how-to and inspirational essays to assist you as you take those first shaky steps toward defining yourself as a writer, or enhancing your existing writing life, and growing your creative voice. As you reach out to other writers and build or reinforce the supportive community of your writing group, you will enrich your life, your art, and our world.

> Good writers define reality; bad ones merely restate it. A good writer turns fact into truth; a bad writer will, more often than not, accomplish the opposite.
> —EDWARD ALBEE

THE

WRITING GROUP

BOOK

PART I

STARTING A WRITING GROUP

■

> **There is no agony
> like bearing an untold story inside of you.**
> —MAYA ANGELOU

How many times have you heard someone say that writing is a lonely process? Writing groups provide a safe, creative environment to explore your writer's voice, collect constructive feedback, and grow as an artist. Whether on-line or in person, both neophyte and experienced writers can benefit from writing groups. Start by exploring the writing groups available to you and if you don't find what you want, create one that suits your needs. Here you'll find how-to and inspirational essays to start you on this journey.

Who? Me? Starting a Writing Group from Scratch

Nancy Viau

~

WRITING GROUP NAME: Write Now!
WRITING GROUP LOCATION: Mullica Hill, New Jersey
TYPE OF WRITERS: Children's writers of fiction and nonfiction, poets, playwrights, and essayists

I BECAME A FAMOUS author at an extremely young age. I felt compelled to pen the adventures of *Shaggy, the Dog*, a picture book about a nearsighted pup, after losing interest in reading material available to me. I confidently distributed my fully illustrated book to the general public. All of my relatives and neighborhood friends exclaimed it to be the best story they ever read! I believed them, of course, and I was proud of my success. However, becoming so well known, and so fast, was a bit daunting. I was a mere six years old. Therefore, I decided to put aside my writing talents to pursue other, perhaps more appropriate, challenges like kickball, tag, and dance. And I went back to reading about Dick, Jane, and Spot.

I did not commit another children's story to paper for quite some time, but I often felt twinges of ideas lurking on the right side of my brain. They surfaced in the form of lesson plans for fourth-graders, and poems or games for students I tutored. Other ideas crept into print as sales pamphlets and newspaper advertisements for a fitness club I managed.

For twenty years I continued to create picture books, fiction, nonfiction, poetry, and essays in my head. Raising four children did nothing to stop new storylines from creeping into everyday thought. My family provided constant inspiration with their funny antics and adventures. Soon my ideas kept me awake at night, and I pondered the thought of someday becoming an author. I remembered the accolades *Shaggy, the Dog* had received thirty-eight years earlier and eventually felt inspired to commit a new picture book idea to paper. I wrote a story about a girl who visited the seashore for the first time. The words poured out from my heart and soul. It was an enjoyable experience, and I knew I was hooked. I wrote and rewrote my story, all the while honing my skill as a neophyte writer.

After several months, I read it to relatives and friends. They loved it! Could it be possible I had written yet another wonderful story? Possible, yes, but not probable. This time I was older and wiser. I had already predicted this positive response because I had not only taken the time to write a story, I had done hours upon hours of research about the writing process. I gleaned information from seasoned authors and editors from their how-to books. I absorbed every bit of information on the Internet I could find. I attended conferences and listened intently to discussions about the writing industry. I had learned that by allowing only relatives and friends read my story, I would not receive absolutely honest opinions about my writing. It was time to follow the advice of the experts: Find or start a critique group and acquire objective feedback on manuscripts.

For several months I looked in my vicinity for a writing group. There were none to be found. I reviewed the idea of starting my own critique group, but the thought *"Who? Me?* I'm not even published!" kept nagging at me. I'm a beginning writer— a newbie (the name I was given by the published writers I met in Web chat rooms). Despite my uneasiness at the possibility of starting and managing a group, I decided to forge ahead. I placed the following advertisement in local libraries, bookstores, and newspapers:

Critique Group

If you are a children's book writer and are interested in sharing ideas, manuscripts, and publishing information in an informal setting, then this is the group for you! Unpublished and published writers, as well as illustrators, are welcome. Call or e-mail for more information.

I received only one response during that first six-week period—a writer who had been working on a manuscript, off and on, for about ten years. We spoke on the phone and decided to get together at my house the following week. I was thrilled that someone was interested in reading my growing number of stories. Our first meeting consisted of getting to know each other and our writing interests. We shared our (often different) thoughts about the writing process and as we departed, we took each other's manuscripts for reviewing. I felt we were on our way to establishing a writing relationship and that other members would soon follow. I never heard from her again. Did she hate my manuscript? Was it so bad that she could not confront me? I'll never know.

Two months passed and I received a second call on my ad. Another writer had noticed it on the library bulletin board and was interested in joining my "group." Again we agreed to meet at my house. I was happy to discover that the person who responded this time, although twenty years my junior, was at exactly the same place in her writing career as I. She had also researched the industry diligently and was actively seeking someone who could help her view her manuscripts with a fresh perspective. She enthusiastically shared books she read and Web sites she found useful. We talked for hours, exchanged manuscripts, and made plans to meet in two weeks at a local bookstore. The days flew by, and I found myself waiting nervously at the bookstore's café. I had thoroughly read my fellow writer's poem and story and offered some encouraging remarks. In addition, I had noted a few areas I thought needed improvement. As I sat there, I hoped my newest group member had done the same for me. Finally, she walked in the door, not only with an armful of books and papers, but also with my marked-up manuscript in her hand. And best of all—she was smiling.

Our group has been through many changes since that time almost three years ago. Several members, including my friend above, have been coming to monthly meetings since the group's inception. Most heard of the group through the advertisement, but several have tagged along with current members to see what we can offer them. Some visited infrequently and eventually stopped attending. These people were enthusiastic about the writing process but felt they didn't have the time to give writing their full attention. We keep them informed through e-mail and hope they will join us again in the future.

Currently, the group mainly consists of children's writers who range from those who have written and submitted many manuscripts to those who are busy working on their first drafts. We are open to reviewing any type of writing at any stage. We are fortunate that among us there are individuals who can offer specific advice because of their expertise in a specialized area: one woman, a theater major in college, gives us insights into iambic pentameter; another, a published essayist, offers ideas on marketing our work. Others contribute by simply sharing their positive and negative responses to our written words. Everyone in the group has benefited from fresh criticism of their manuscripts given in a friendly, nonthreatening manner.

Although none of us are published children's book authors, a few are making progress. We leave each session with a renewed sense of purpose and look forward to meeting again. We realize that although we appreciate all those compliments from family and friends, we rely on our group to help us laugh at our mistakes, improve our writing, and encourage us to celebrate all our published and unpublished accomplishments.

Favorite Resources

BOOKS

Balkin, Richard. *A Writer's Guide to Book Publishing*. New York, NY: Penguin Books, Inc., 1994.

Fife, Bruce. *An Insider's Guide to Getting Published*. Colorado Springs, CO: Piccadilly Books, 1995.

Pope, Alice. *Children's Writers and Illustrators Market*. Cincinnati, OH: Writer's Digest Books, 2001.

Sebranek, Patrick; Verne Meyer; and Dave Kemper. *Writers Inc.: A Student Handbook for Writing and Learning*. Wilmington, MA: Houghton Mifflin, 1996.

Seuling, Barbara. *How to Write a Children's Book and Get It Published*. New York: MacMillian General Reference, A Simon & Shuster MacMillan Company, 1991.

WEB SITES

www.cbcbooks.org

www.institutechildrenslit.com

www.rhymezone.com

www.scbwi.org

www.write4kids.com

www.writersdigest.com

www.writing-world.com

> **Any writer worth the name is always getting into one thing or getting out of another thing.**
> —FANNIE HURST

Sailing the Cyber-Seas

*How to Start an On-Line Writing Group
Without Getting Seasick*

Jason Groom

~

WRITING GROUP NAME: Revenge of the Sally Mae
WRITING GROUP LOCATION: Chicago, Illinois
TYPE OF WRITERS: Short fiction and playwrights

Bloomsbury. It is the first word that comes to me when someone mentions a writing group. It conjures up images of formal settings, of parlors and sitting rooms, of E. M. Forster and Virginia Woolf. The only problem is—and this will get me in trouble with my former English professor—I don't really like Virginia Woolf. There is more to a writing group than this. Writing groups are places where authors can come together to explore language and themes with like-minded individuals. They are collectives that can help sharpen skills and develop voice, and the advent of the Internet has made them more useful than ever before. So, how do we get beyond the image of Desmond MacCarthy sitting with his legs crossed, his tan socks showing, and a cup of tea resting on the table at arm's length as he expounds on the virtue of his latest artistic find?

How do we escape into the electronic world of chat rooms and bulletin boards without being haunted by Ms. Woolf and her lighthouse?

We begin with a metaphor to give us focus and direction. By collecting our thoughts under one unifying allegory, one flag if you will, we are able to keep our efforts from spiraling out of control. Without a theme, we would soon be set adrift, a crew without a ship, a ship without stars to steer by, a . . . I think you get the point.

So let's say we are pirates. It's as good an image as any. We are cutthroat bandits, literary privateers hell-bent on the gold and glory, sailing the cyber seas; and like all good pirates, our flag flies high over the deck of our ship.

"What ship?" you ask.

Good question. The symbolism is important to the overall feel of the group. It gives structure to the otherwise noncorporeal potential that is the Internet. Technical questions can be turned into creative challenges as you try to fit each problem into the framework of the theme. What kind of Web site do we want? What kind of ship do we need? How fast is our connection? How many pirates are we going to have? What about real-time chats? Do we want to recruit? Who will we recruit? Will there be alliances with other pirates? Do you want FTP access? See how the questions begin to take shape when you add the metaphor?

The ship is a good place to start. There are a lot of different Web-hosting services available, and what you get depends on how much you want to spend. The more you pay, the more amenities your ship will have. Let's say that we are cheap and that we do not want to spend any money—we *are* pirates after all. The Internet is a great resource for the cheap at heart and

there are many places where you can find free turnkey com-
munities. The best place to go when looking for a free host site
is where you find free e-mail. On-line providers of free e-mail
(Yahoo, MSN, Lycos, and so on) are often set up to supply all
the necessary services you need; however, they do differ in what
utilities are available, so browse the sites, checking the sails and
anchors, before making your final choice.

Now we have chosen our ship. We went to Lycos.com and
browsed the clubs. We got a good deal on a small dinghy. It's not
loaded with bells and whistles, but it is upgradeable and gives
each pirate a little privacy. There is a main meeting area and
room to add polls, both are standard options that can be found
in almost any site, and will fit our needs for now. As with many
free on-line providers, there is also an option to upgrade to a
paid site if the need arises. The paid sites expand the amount of
memory available and will allow for a seamless transition from
a two-bit thug to the scourge of the literary world. As we break
the bottle and release the moorings, the HMS *Metaphorical
Marauder* slips out of the harbor. What's next?

The thing our pirate ship needs more than anything else
(save maybe the ship itself) is a crew. We need pirates. Putting
together and running a writing group requires participation, so
getting people to join you is key. Most of the preconstructed
sites will come with a way to invite people to join your ranks.
Our ship comes with a small communications lobby just below
the lido deck and from there I send out the message.

Here is where the need for analogies and metaphors really
starts to play a role. When sending out the first message to
friends and colleagues, you are setting the tone for the rest of
the conversations to come. If I stick to the analogy of a pirate's
ship, throwing in a "starboard" here and an "avast, ye matey"

there, I can focus the group. Role playing and overall symbolism create cohesion that may not be available to a more conventional writing group.

Just because you have gotten people to join the crew does
not ensure their participation. This is one of the largest setbacks
to any kind of writing group, but even more so for on-line com-
munities. The idea is to get people together so they can share
their work, but if they never participate, what is the point? One
way of getting people to participate is to give them roles. Assign
one person to be the communications officer, someone else
to be the sergeant-at-arms. You can assign a liaison to foreign
dignitaries, or an entertainer; any title will work to focus the
attentions of your crew while adding depth to the underlying
storyline and characters.

This also brings up a unique characteristic of the on-line
writing group. The persona, or voice, one uses on the Web is
called an avatar. It is like method acting in that it allows the
writer to become anyone he or she wants to be. The role the
writer takes on becomes internalized as she or he slips into the
character and develops a greater feeling for the fictitious personality. The avatar frees the writer from self-censorship and
releases him or her from inhibitions. By taking on the manner-
isms of another, the writer can express controversial opinions
with fewer repercussions.

Now we've found a ship and the crew is coming from far and
wide to raise the sails and man the cannons, but where are these
sails and what are the cannons? That is up to the captain. As
with any metaphor, the true power is in the hands of the creator.
Web sites like this one are made to allow people to interact on
many different levels, so many in fact that it is often hard to get

people to use any media—chat rooms, bulletin boards (BBS), file transfer programs (FTP), and so on—other than the one they are most used to. By injecting a bit of creative electricity and putting your members on the metaphoric hot seat, a Web-based writing group like this can unleash the potential of all involved. It allows people to explore their writing and themselves. Turn the discussion board into a sewing room, a place where the crew can come to add thoughts to a growing tapestry that will be both our wind and sails; in the chat room, use questions as weapons for verbal sparring; and of course, no ship would be complete without a main mast where the pirates can hoist their ideas high enough for the whole world to see.

In the end, we have an oceanworthy vessel. We have a place where people can come together to share their thoughts and find new ideas, where they can stretch their imaginations or just get away. A pirate ship may not be what everyone thinks of when putting together a writing group. I would be hard-pressed to imagine Virginia Woolf with a peg leg and a knife between her teeth, but that is what makes the Internet work. Not all writers out there are Virginia Woolf, and not all writing groups have to be like Bloomsbury.

Favorite Resources

The following links are just a few of the on-line places for the aspiring artist. As with any market, look through past issues for an idea of what they are looking for. Always remember to follow your instincts. If you think you have a piece that will work with a specific journal, follow through; you can always come back to the links later.

WEB SITES

www.forwriters.com
This is a great site for market listings.

www.conjunctions.com
This is the Internet form for the Bard College Review (no
e-submissions).

www.3rdbed.com
This site features literature, poetry, and hypertext.

www.webdelsol.com
Here's an Internet magazine along the lines of *Poets & Writers*.

www.altx.com/index2.html
This is an Internet magazine with a high-tech concentration.

www.clamcity.com/eotu.html
This site features poetry and fiction with illustrations. (This site
was not so gothic when I first found it.)

http://opticmagazine.com
This one is postmodern with a lean toward pop culture. Non-
genre fiction, poetry, and nonfiction. Currently the site is not
taking submissions.

http://pifmagazine.com/2001/02
This Internet magazine is full of fiction, nonfiction, and poetry.

www.3ammagazine.com/index.html
This is a well-rounded Internet magazine—fiction, nonfiction,
poetry, and political essays.

www.melicreview.com
This Internet magazine has a concentration on poetry.

www.6ftferrets.com
As it says, writing group; more conventional.
(Note: An essay from a member of this writing group begins on page 190.)

www.nwu.org
This is a great Web site for the freelance writers union.

www.chicagowriter.com
Here's a resource for Chicago writers.

www.randomhouse.com/knopf/home.html
This is an on-line journal from Knopf. (I like it because of the dog.)

> When I face the desolate impossibility of writing 500 pages, a sick sense of failure falls on me, and I know I can never do it. Then gradually, I write one page and then another. One day's work is all I can permit myself to contemplate.
> —JOHN STEINBECK

Writing from the Heartland

*How to Maintain a Screenwriting Group
2,000 Miles from Hollywood*

Eric Diekhans

~

WRITING GROUP NAME: Chicago Screenwriters' Group
WRITING GROUP LOCATION: Chicago, Illinois
TYPE OF WRITERS: Screenwriters

IT WAS A DARK and stormy night, metaphorically speaking.
Six of us, all aspiring screenwriters, were gathered at the Perfect Cup, a cozy neighborhood café on Chicago's North Side.
We were a gloomy, woeful bunch. Behind us, the Tuesday night knitters were loud and lively. We could hardly hear ourselves think. Not that we were entertaining pleasant thoughts. Week after week of writing and rewriting and rewriting again for the thirteenth time and none of us seemed near that most elusive of goals—the first sale. Thanks in no small measure to the group's feedback, we had polished our screenplays until they gleamed, but they still weren't what the producers and agents wanted. They were looking for edgy but safe, original but familiar. By the end of the evening, we were threatening to give Hollywood a collective middle finger and seek solace in knitting needles and

yarn. Maybe we could finish a cozy scarf or crewneck before another bitter Chicago winter arrived.

Our group had begun its life five years previously as a workshop at Cinestory, a national screenwriters' organization. Pam Pierce, Cinestory's cofounder, coaxed us through our first attempts to dissect and improve each other's scripts. We were green—most of us had completed only one or two scripts—so Pam did most of the talking.

When our twelve weeks were up we decided to continue on our own. I thought we were all dedicated to the same cause—becoming professional screenwriters. But without the incentive of knowing we were paying for the opportunity to workshop, the level of commitment quickly waned. Three or four meetings into our experiment there were only two of us left—Diane Berz, a playwright turned screenwriter, and myself.

I love the concept of the writing group. As writer Julia Cameron puts it, "We belong to an ancient and holy tribe." I love the idea of gathering much like our ancestors did, minus the campfire, to share stories and release our collective energy. I love the sense of camaraderie, the discipline of a regular deadline, the thrill of hearing my words read aloud for the first time, the pleasure of welcoming a talented new scribe into our midst.

I jumped in and decided I would be the one to resurrect our sinking ship. The trouble was, I didn't know the first thing about organizing a writing group. I'd never even belonged to one before. But how hard could it be?

Damn hard, I soon discovered. Maybe in L.A., where screenwriters swarm the cafés like medflies on an orange grove; people there are beating down the doors to join a screenwriting group. But here in the Midwest, people are too busy with real work. The most frequent response I get when I tell a Chicago native that I'm a screenwriter is an incredulous, "You can make money at that?"

But I knew that there had to be more of us out there. The perfect opportunity for first contact came when a script I developed in Pam's workshop was named a semifinalist in the Illinois/Chicago Screenplay Competition. All the writers who had advanced were invited to a screenwriting workshop. Here would be some thirty screenwriters, presumably with at least a modicum of ability, who would jump at a chance to be part of our group. Near the end of the workshop I stood up and extolled the benefits of belonging to a screenwriting group. I was like a Baptist preacher offering a key to the gates of heaven and warning of the pitfalls of writing in isolation. I expected people to flock around me after the meeting, excitedly asking for my number. Instead, the assembled talent made a quick exit to the elevators. Only two people stopped to say they were interested.

It seems a lot of writers like the isolation. That's why we're writers instead of wedding planners. Outside of the Hollywood madhouse, it's easy to be in isolation—no pitch meetings, no story conferences, no glamorous premieres.

Commitment is also a big issue for screenwriters working far away from Tinsel Town. After months of posting messages on screenwriting newsgroups and at the Cinestory offices, and talking up the group wherever I went, I had developed a decent list of e-mail addresses of interested writers. Many of them would show up for a few meetings; they seemed to be working hard on their scripts. But then they would disappear. Fearing that we were doing something wrong, I e-mailed them to ask why they'd stopped coming. While a few writers were working on their own film projects or just found our meeting time or location inconvenient, their number one excuse was that they had stopped writing.

I know that there are probably many writers in L.A. who haven't touched their keyboard in months, but there's a certain level of pressure that comes from living in L.A. that you don't get in Chicago. If you move to Southern California to become a screenwriter then you'd damn well better be writing. The guilt weighs heavy. Everyone you meet is connected with the industry. Some of them are actually getting a paycheck. You should be too. On the other hand, if you're a Chicago screenwriter who's not writing, it just means you've come to your senses.

Undaunted, I continued to market our group at every opportunity. At one meeting twelve writers showed up. At others, it was just Diane and me staring at one another across the table and wondering if this was worth it.

It was. Every writer who attended regularly saw at least some improvement. Our scripts were placing in contests and even getting nibbles from producers and agents.

As the group developed we learned what was most conducive to success. After first meeting in our homes, then at a hip tearoom that went belly up, Diane suggested relocating to the Perfect Cup. It was kitty-corner from an El stop and had reasonable street parking, a combination that's rare in Chicago. Anne, the owner, and her sister, Christina, who worked our shift, made us feel welcome. Unlike Hollywood directors, they liked having a bunch of screenwriters hanging around, even when we played roles that required us to shout brutal threats at one another. When Ann decided to close early during the long winter she even let us continue our meetings after hours. I guess those generous tips we left paid off.

Through trial and error we determined how frequently we should convene. Some L.A. groups meet every week, but those are for people writing full-time. Here, every three weeks seems to work well. We encourage group members to bring in ten to twenty pages of whatever they're working on. Twenty pages translate into a page a day over three weeks. That's doable even for a writer working a demanding job.

Because beggars can't be choosers, we don't discriminate about who can join. While Diane and I have each written several screenplays and even optioned scripts we developed in the group, many of the writers who show up are even greener than we were when we took Pam's workshop. But sometimes even a person who has never typed "fade in" at the top of a page may still provide insights that can transform a good script into a great one. In turn, we just might inspire that person to take the risk of putting a story onto the page.

Three weeks after that dark and stormy night, the knitters were back and so were we, maybe not full of high hopes, but at least with another twenty pages under our belts. Whether you're writing in Hollywood or in Chicago, that counts for something.

> **Develop interest in life as you see it; in people, things, literature, music—the world is so rich, simply throbbing with rich treasures, beautiful souls and interesting people. Forget yourself.**
> —HENRY MILLER

The Workplace Writing Group

TINA MARIE SMITH

~

WRITING GROUP NAME: Authors Round Table
WRITING GROUP LOCATION: Orlando, Florida
TYPE OF WRITERS: Fiction writers working on novel-length projects, children's writers, playwrights, and role-playing game writers

A WRITING GROUP provides a wonderful support system for a writer who holds down a "real job" during the day and writes at night. But not all writing groups are structured to help writers balance their work and writing life. For writers struggling to find time to write, much less attend another meeting during their workweek, the workplace writing group may be the best solution.

I live in a fairly large city where half a dozen writing groups compete for attention and attendance. I belong to a small, spoiled group that has been in existence a dozen years. Yes, spoiled. Some of our members recently went on a fact-finding mission to one of the larger groups in our area and came back to report the existence of something called dues. We wondered if we should charge dues, but we couldn't figure out what we'd do with the money. Our meeting space is comfortable and fully equipped. We have access to more audio and video equipment than we can use. We advertise in a newspaper with a circulation of 50,000 people, and our information is on a Web site with an audience of more than 100,000 people. All this is free. We're taking advantage of our corporate culture. We work at the Walt Disney World Resort, and as I've said, we're spoiled.

If you're thinking of starting a writing group, consider the advantages of meeting where you work.

- **Being there.** The big challenge for any writing group is keeping members coming. If you meet at work, most people have already invested their time in the daily commute. They are already there. The writing group is an extra hour or two tacked on to the end of the day or squeezed into a lunch break.

- **Meeting space and advertising.** Many companies have meeting space, training space, cafeterias, or other facilities that can be made available to employees, often at no cost. Many companies will promote clubs in the company newsletter, on the company Intranet site, or on bulletin boards in cafeterias and break areas.

- **A common bond.** Who are these people you'll be sharing your work with? The workplace connection can help establish a level of professionalism and trust in the writing group. Our membership includes published writers and developing writers. Many of our members have taught college-level courses in topics including fiction writing, journalism, and theater arts.

- **Networking.** Double-duty your time. Combine your company and writing networking opportunities. While working to write that novel, you may find other opportunities. We have writing group members who've written articles for the company newsletter, provided content for company Web sites, and even written educational programs for cruise ships.

Where to Start

When you're trying to start your writing group, here are some questions to consider.

- **The company culture.** Does the company environment allow for the sharing of a variety of writing styles and topics? If not, you may need to structure the group according to a certain type of writing or find a meeting place outside the company.

- **Size.** Is your workplace large enough to support an ongoing writing group? How large do you want your group to be? I've known writing groups that were fifty members strong and groups that consisted of three friends who discussed their latest projects over lunch. Both can be helpful to your development as a writer, but if you only want to share with a couple of friends, you may not need to establish a formal writing group.

- **Company policies.** Does your workplace have a policy for establishing clubs and groups? In most large companies, you can check with the human resources department for information. At a minimum, most companies will expect groups to follow the nondiscrimination and noncompetitive policies. Nondiscrimination policies may include age and gender discrimination, so you may not be able to form the Female Romance Writers or the Senior Scribblers for writers over sixty. You must also be willing to accept anyone with an interest in writing, regardless of ability. Noncompetitive agreements mean this isn't the place to work on the tell-all book about your company. But be aware of company policies that may apply to your writing even if you don't form a group. Writing done for your company newsletter or on company time may be considered "work for hire," which belongs to the company. Also, some companies may provide the facilities but not allow the use of the company name as part of the club's name.

- **Meeting space.** Your company may provide meeting space at no cost, but the trade-off may be the possibility of being moved or canceled if the space is needed for business purposes.

- **Advertising.** Does your company have a newsletter, Web site, bulletin boards, or other space where you can advertise your writing group?

- **Nonemployees.** Does the company have a policy regarding allowing nonemployees to join the group? If someone leaves the company, can they continue with the group? This may not seem like a problem until the mystery writer leaves just before revealing the murderer.

The First Meeting

Eventually most of your members will want to share their work, but first everyone will need to become acquainted. Your first meeting should be more structured, perhaps with a guest speaker or panel discussion on a general writing topic, such as how to get published. Prepare an information handout explaining how the group will work. I don't recommend exchanging writing to be critiqued yet. For the second meeting, have another topic of discussion or some writing exercise to share. Don't be surprised to find fewer attendees at your second meeting than you had at the first. You're now narrowing it down to those who have a real interest in the group. If you're going to include critiquing as part of your group structure, you can start the exchange process during this meeting. Be prepared to be the first to offer up your work or have a friend ready to hand out his/her work. Want to bring people back? Start with the first chapter of a suspense-filled novel. All writers are readers. We want to know what happens next.

Regardless of the size of the group or the skill of the individual members, a writing group can be an invaluable source of support as you pursue your writing career. There is no greater encouragement than a reader eagerly awaiting your next creative effort.

> **The man who doesn't read good books has no advantage over the man who can't read them.**
> —MARK TWAIN

Somehow, the Scenes Still Happen

Writing in the Round

E. A. Bagby

~

WRITING GROUP NAME: Spinkleteen

WRITING GROUP LOCATION: Chicago, Illinois

TYPE OF WRITERS: Sketch comedy writers with playwriting and screenwriting backgrounds

L ET'S TALK for a moment about fear.

Fear is probably endemic to writers. William Gass, in *Finding a Form*, discusses the childhood anxieties that led him to write, and continues: "Make no mistake, writing puts the writer in illusory command of the world, empowers someone otherwise powerless." We're afraid of what we can't control—which is, let's face it, nearly everything—so we create imaginary events and control them instead.

But sometimes fear prevents creativity as much as it stimulates it. One writer friend guards her manuscripts so closely that she never lets them out of her control. She rarely submits, revises for years, never finishes. Working as an editor—witnessing the absurdities to which the unguarded pen is prone, fretting that she has committed worse—hasn't helped. All right, fine: the "friend" is me. I've always been a perfectionist, which is a nice way of saying control freak. In fact, to be completely honest, in my desk are no fewer than three novels, never published, never submitted, finished but not *finished*. Am I afraid? Yes. Abjectly.

It is not unfounded, as we all know. Obscurity, penury—these are valid, concrete fears for the writer, and they, along with rejection itself, are the reasons we don't handle rejection so well. Still, we must not let them get the upper hand.

Lately, I've learned a way to master those fears, and it's come from the last place I expected it: my sketch comedy troupe.

I've been in other troupes, and they always worked the same way: One or two people wrote scenes on their own and brought them to the troupe, and if enough of us liked something we'd assign parts and start rehearsing it. But with Spinkleteen (the name came from a gibberish sketch at an early writing session) everything is different.

The six of us sit around a table. Each has a legal pad and a pen. Usually some sort of music is playing; the *Rushmore* soundtrack and Herbie Hancock are popular. Each of us writes six lines of a scene and passes the legal pad to the right. Then we read the scenes we've just received and add six lines to those. Then we pass again, and so on, until each of us has worked on every scene. At the end of the session we read the scenes aloud, and people volunteer to type and revise the ones that interest them. When a sketch is finished, beneath the title is the byline: *By the Collective*.

This is clearly an unacceptable lack of control over my words.

At my first meeting—when I learned how the troupe wrote—I panicked. I wrote a line, loosely construable as dialogue, and didn't even attribute it to a character. Tom, who was next to me that night, gave me a strange look, added a character's name to my line, and went on with the scene. Then I looked at the page I'd been given and began to catch on. By the end of the session it felt, well, oddly comfortable. Probably my psychological process was akin to what many women experienced when it became permissible not to wear corsets in polite company.

One benefit is immediately apparent: This is the first time I've been in a troupe with no divas. We've all invested equally in the scenes. No one will storm out of the room if a given sketch isn't in the next show. No one is the stahhhh. We are the Collective.

Another benefit: When the legal pads are making their rounds and the people to either side of you are silently mouthing dialogue, *not* writing is simply not an option. Writer's block, you realize, is a luxury for people who have the time to obsess about it. When all you must do is continue a scene, no matter how bad the lines are, you find a way to write them. You "just keep the thing going any way you can," as Tennessee Williams said. And the next time you're stumped in your own work, try writing just six more lines. Can you do that? Try six more. They may not be right—we've come up with plenty of clunkers—but they'll be there, and at least they'll show you what wrong looks like.

A third benefit, miraculous and liberating, is the discovery that we all write good lines and we all write bad lines. Writing in the round, you learn very quickly that no one's penmanship is perfect, no one's hyphenation is up to *Chicago Manual of Style* standards, and no one's wit sparkles unfailingly. (In fact, you often don't even know when you've started a joke; it's just another detail until the next writer brings it back with a twist.

So you stop worrying about being funny, which—surprise!—makes it a whole lot easier to be funny.)

Finally, we are friends, and we are closer because of this work. We trust each other with the mistakes, the outbursts, the frustrations, the things many people spend their lives trying to hide. Sometimes we meet at the end of days that have exhausted us, pummeled us, mugged us, cheated us, fired us—and somehow the scenes still happen. Together, we write. Alone, we'd never write the same things. Some nights, alone, we wouldn't write at all.

Now, I am not suggesting that you run off and start a sketch comedy troupe to allay your insecurities about your novel. If you need to write sketch comedy, you'll know, just as you knew you needed to write fiction; odds are you're already doing it. But try bringing a stack of legal pads to the next meeting of your writers group. Try writing a short story, a chapter, or a movie scene in the round. Try letting go—releasing your work to survive and grow in the wild.

You'll rediscover your own strengths and weaknesses. You'll learn that the woman to your right has an instinct for story structure, which means maybe she can help you coax your stubborn hero into a scene. Most important, you'll write. And you'll get used to being read by others, which is the point, isn't it?

Favorite Resources

BOOKS

Borges, Jorge Luis. *This Craft of Verse*. Cambridge, MA: Harvard University Press, 2000.

Calvino, Italo. *Six Memos for the Next Millennium*. Translated by
Patrick Creagh. New York: Vintage International, 1988.

Dillard, Annie. *The Writing Life*. New York: HarperPerennial, 1989.

Gardner, John. *The Art of Fiction*. New York: Vintage Books, 1991.

King, Stephen. *On Writing: A Memoir of the Craft*. New York:
Scribner, 2000.
I never expected to like this nearly as much as I do now. It's given
me a whole new respect for the man. For someone just starting
out or someone who wants to reconnect with the basics, it's
terrific—plain talk about what writing demands of you.

Lamott, Anne. *Bird by Bird: Some Instructions on Writing and
Life*. New York: Anchor Books, 1995.
This is probably on every list, isn't it?

Strunk, William Jr., E. B. White, and Roger Angell. *The Elements of
Style*. Fourth edition. Boston, MA: Allyn & Bacon, 2000.
I read this book about once a year.

*Finally, for anyone who wants to write for theater, I'd recom-
mend learning about the other people who make a play happen.
Here are some good places to start:*

Callow, Simon. *Being an Actor*. New York: St. Martin's Griffin,
1984.

Hagen, Uta, with Haskell Frankel. *Respect for Acting*. New York:
Hungry Minds, Inc., New York, 1973.

Stanislavski, Constantin. *An Actor Prepares*. Translated by
Elizabeth Reynolds Hapgood. New York: Routledge, 1936.

Sweet, Jeffrey. *Something Wonderful Right Away*. New York: Limelight Editions, 1989.

Of course, it is impossible to read too much, or to see too much theater.

WEB SITE

www.egoproductions.org/spinkleteen

> One of the few things I know about writing is this: spend it all, shoot it, play it, lose it, all, right away, every time. Do not hoard what seems good for a better place in the book, or for another book; give it, give it all, give it now.
> —ANNIE DILLARD, *The Writing Life*

A Story Circle for Women

RENEE HOWARD CASSESE

~

WRITING GROUP NAME: Women's Story Circle
WRITING GROUP LOCATION: Seaford, New York
TYPE OF WRITERS: Life writers and essayists

> We are, each of us, our own prisoner.
> We are locked up in our own story.
> —MAXINE KUMIN

WOMEN'S STORIES have for years been silenced, or written by men who cannot interpret them with any degree of accuracy. The world needs to hear these stories, and more importantly, women need to write them. In order to facilitate this need, women across the country and around the world are forming story circles. A story circle is a group of women who come together to write their life stories, read and share them with the group, and read and discuss the published stories and memoirs of other women. In the process we discover not only things about ourselves, but how uniquely bonded each of us is to all women.

Starting a story circle is a way to help women fulfill the need to validate and make sense of their lives. You can begin with a group of women you know, or you may start out on your own. Story circles may sprout up at women's clubs, in libraries, or at local bookstores, any of which can provide a meeting place. Some circles meet in the homes of the members, alternating week to week in each home. Some may begin as a class in an adult education program, with a facilitator to lead the writing and discussions.

A story circle can include whatever activities the members agree on, but a highly productive and workable format can go something like this. Sessions will run from two to three hours during which the women will engage in timed writing exercises. A prompt will be given and a timer or piece of music will be used to designate the time for writing. After the timed writing, which can be from five to twenty minutes, the women will read and discuss their stories. This is risky business. Though stories may be written about any part of our lives, and express emotions of joy, pain, love, fear, sorrow, and more, it is the intense feelings and experiences we most need to write about. Each member will choose how much she wants to share with her circle, but those who explore the dark corners of their lives, and allow other women into those hidden spaces, will find a sea of acceptance and support. Often story circle members are surprised to find out how many other women have experienced the same or similar trials and tribulations.

Women who are members of a story circle are not only bonded by the sharing of their stories, but also by a pact of trust within the group. We trust each other not to disclose the truths that are exposed within the Women's Story Circle and we trust each other to be supportive and uncritical in discussing our stories. When we venture into the risky business of sharing our dark shadows we need trustworthy companions on the journey into our own hearts and souls. We find these companions in the story circles that women today are giving birth to.

We can find support and acceptance too in the memoirs of other women. When we read the memoirs of other women we see that our truths, as well as our lies, are close to being universal. We find solace and strength in knowing that many women have lived and survived the same traumas and dark thoughts that we have.

In discussing the stories that women in the circle share we establish rules for comment, the most important being a promise of gentility. If members wish to publish their work, then we can discuss the mechanics of writing. Otherwise, we come together to share the experiences of our lives, and these are not right or wrong, good or bad, they simply are. It is not for us to judge each other, but to comment on the emotional side of the story and to validate each member's life as having meaning and purpose. The process is enlightening and rewarding and stirs the soul.

Writers are a unique group and when they are women, their stories are uniquely individual and universal at the same time. As we explore these stories we find a place for ourselves among other women, as women and as writers. We find in our stories the hearts and souls of what it means to be a woman. Some of the prompts we use to call up the stories of our lives are:

- Write a story about your birth.

- List all the homes you've lived in. Which has the happiest memory? The darkest?

- Write about an important lesson you have learned.

- Write about a time you did something you shouldn't have done.

- Make a list of your achievements.

- Write about the birth of your first child. Or an adoption. Or why you didn't or couldn't have children.

- Describe your ideal place to live.

- Describe your ideal day.

Writing under the pressure of time has frustrated some story circle members, but it also forces them to silence the inner critic who cries, "You can't write about that!" or "Is that the word you really want to use?" The inner critic can stifle our abilities to express ourselves fully. In our circles we try to shut that critic up as much as possible.

$\sim$

Starting or joining a story circle is a risk, but it's one well worth taking. Women who thought they couldn't write find that indeed they can. They can also face the demons that live inside them. The most reluctant story writer is often the first to suggest that the sessions should last longer than their allotted time. After the conclusion of a six-week series of story circles, they want to continue to meet with their trusted new writing friends. While you contemplate the possibility of starting your own story circle try this writing exercise:

What is the one story about your life that you most want to tell? Why do you need to tell it? How would it help you to share this story with other women? How would it help you if you heard a similar story written by another woman? How would you like to start a story circle?

Favorite Resources

BOOKS

Albert, Susan Wittig. *Writing from Life: Telling Your Soul's Story*.
New York: G. P. Putnam's Sons, 1996.
Especially for women who want to write the stories of their
lives, this is an essential guidebook for getting deep into one's
self development.

Cameron, Julia. *The Artist's Way*. New York: G. P. Putnam's Sons,
1992.
This book will silence your inner critic and jump-start your creative power.

Reeves, Judy. *A Writer's Book of Days*. Novato, California: New
World Library, 1999.
This one contains a lot of inspiration and information for writ-
ers. A year's worth of prompts that can be applied to any genre.

ORGANIZATIONS

STORY CIRCLE NETWORK
P.O. Box 500127
Austin, Texas 78750
www.storycircle.org
This national network of women writing their life stories was
founded by the author of *Writing from Life*, Susan Wittig Albert.
A quarterly journal of writings from its members and a Web site
chock-full of information and resources. Includes e-circles for
writing life stories and reading published memoirs written by
women.

An Expatriate's Guide to Writing Groups

Lawrence Schimel

~

WRITING GROUP NAME: Spain Chapter of Society of Children's Book Writers and Illustrators (SCBWI) and Madrid Poets
WRITING GROUP LOCATION: Madrid, Spain
TYPE OF WRITERS: Children's book writers and illustrators and English-speaking poets

M OST OF US have a romantic Bohemian idea of the life of an expatriate writer, usually summed up by this image: sitting in a street-side café, scribbling longhand in a notebook. Perhaps these days our mental image might be updated to exchange the notebook for a laptop computer, but one thing remains the same: while there may be many people in the background, the expatriate writer is sitting at that café table alone.

I'd been living in Madrid, Spain, for more than two years before I began to really notice the absence of a community of writing peers. I was, of course, in communication with many writer friends and colleagues via the Internet, but interaction with a handful of flesh-and-blood human beings who talk the same talk you do (not just in terms of speaking English, but also understanding the jargon of writing) and who can empathize with the struggles you're going through (be they wrestling with the muse on a specific text or arguing over contract terms for your latest accepted work) is a unique, irreplaceable experience.

I am now involved in both an English-language shop-talk group and a traditional writer's critique group, and both serve different necessary functions in my life, both as a writer and an expat. I hope my personal experiences with different kinds of writing groups will help you find or build your own community, no matter where you find yourself in the world.

Join an Existing Group or Start Your Own?

Chances are, an English-language writing group of some kind already exists in your area. Especially if you will only be living abroad for a short period of time, it's easiest to join someone else's group because starting a group usually takes time. One of the most important factors in getting a group started successfully is regular meetings, on a set schedule, and in a steady venue, which can be publicly announced. If you, as coordinator, have started a group but won't be able to make it on a given month, deputize one of the other regular members to run the session on that same regular date. This lets new members find your group.

Think about your needs as a writer. Are you looking more to share marketing advice and editorial war stories, or do you want hands-on help with your manuscripts?

One of the groups I belong to in Madrid, an English-language poetry group, is an offshoot of an English-language mixed-genre group. While the poets (who are generally also fiction *readers* even if they don't also write prose themselves) were able to critique the stories and novel chunks, they felt that the fiction writers didn't understand their work, or weren't able to offer useful suggestions. So they started a new group, to better meet the specific needs of poets.

The other group I belong to is the bilingual Spanish chapter of the Society of Children's Book Writers and Illustrators (SCBWI), which I was asked to start when I innocently asked the SCBWI international coordinator if there were other members here in Spain.

Where to Find or Announce a Group

I found my critique group by accident when I was trying to publicize the children's book group. There are various national or regional English-language publications covering either Spain in general (such as *The Broadsheet*) or specific cities/regions (the monthly *In Madrid* or the weekly *Sur in English* covering all of Andalucia). This is likely to be the case in other Western-friendly countries. Many of them offer free classifieds, which is both how I found my poetry group and how most new members or visitors find the children's book group.

Here are some other ideas for recruiting writers or finding a group that meets your needs:

- There are English-language Web sites for many countries, which may post announcements.

- Post notices at international bookshops. Madrid has both a secondhand and a new international bookstore, both of which have bulletin boards.

- Check out universities, both local and English-speaking universities with study-abroad programs.

- There may be an American School (or equivalent) nearby. Try contacting the librarian, who may be interested and supportive. Parents of students may also be potential members.

- Contact the local U.S./U.K./Australian embassies/consulates, which may have newsletters for their nationals in that country.

- Contact the local Fulbright office.

- Check for local U.S. Army bases.

- Check for organizations like an American Women's Club, International Newcomer's Club, and so forth.

Where to Hold Your Meetings

Especially when starting a group, choose neutral public spaces to meet. Once you have a regular group going and decide to close it to new members, you can switch to meeting in people's homes.

An American Library or American School (or equivalent) might allow you to use its space—or you may discover existing groups already doing so and decide to join forces.

For the SCBWI Spain group, a children's bookstore offered us free use of its downstairs space. [Editor's note: This is a good tip for people starting a group in the United States as well.] The relationship works out well for all of us. New members attracted to the group can discover a store specializing in the kinds of books they're interested in writing and/or illustrating, the store is regularly mentioned in all of our announcements, and during meetings we have close at hand a lot of the books we mention or recommend (or wrote or illustrated!).

For the poetry group, we meet at a café. It's not an official arrangement, and sometimes our habitual table has already been claimed by another group, but it works out well enough, and as long as we each order a drink, they let us stay for a few hours. It's not on a sidewalk, but we're doing our part to uphold that timeless Bohemian image of the expatriate writer!

English-Only or Bilingual?

Chances are that even if you decide on an English-only group, you'll find yourselves collectively puzzling over Britishisms, Australianisms, American slang from other parts of the country than where you've lived, and so forth. Especially for a critique group, I'd advise restricting the group to native English speakers only; this lets you concentrate on the writing itself and suggestions for making each piece better, instead of dealing with locals who want to practice their English skills.

The children's book group is part of a larger organization. These meetings are not critique groups but more social sessions (during which members sometimes decide to form critique groups that meet at other times), so we make do with the varying levels of English or Spanish competence. The group is also divided among illustrators and writers, yet another nightmare for the coordinator in terms of planning speakers and events that address everyone's needs, but we're all united by our love of children's books. The more focused your group is, the more likely it will fulfill your needs.

Short-Term Members?

Many of the general concerns about writing groups covered elsewhere in this volume apply to an expatriate group. One additional concern for overseas groups is that interested writers may only be visiting for a period of weeks or months. High turnover of members is usually disruptive in a writing group, especially for fiction writers working on longer pieces. Depending on how often you meet, and how the group is set up, short-term visitors may or may not be welcome. Are visitors allowed to submit work? If you have a core of regulars, these transient new faces and voices may be an interesting diversion. These are questions each group must decide on its own.

Since the children's book group is a chapter of an existing international organization (the SCBWI has more than 16,000 members worldwide), United States–based members who find themselves overseas, even for a short time, are already tapped into a community of writing peers.

Back to That Street-Side Café

I hope the muse inspires you, sitting there writing in that street-side café, and that when you need the input of your peers, these suggestions help you find or create a supportive writing community overseas.

Favorite Resources

www.underdown.org
The Purple Crayon

www.smartwriters.com
Smart Writers

www.scbwi.org
Society of Children's Book Writers and Illustrators

www.verlakay.com
Verla Kay's Web site

Group Effort

Organizing a Family of Writers

Richard Holinger

~

WRITING GROUP NAME: St. Charles Writers Group
WRITING GROUP LOCATION: Geneva, Illinois
TYPE OF WRITERS: Poets, playwrights, novelists, short fiction writers, essayists, creative nonfiction writers, memoirists

S EVEN YEARS AGO, after giving a poetry workshop supported in part by the Illinois Arts Council and sponsored by the St. Charles Public Library, I was asked by enthusiastic patrons to facilitate an ongoing creative writing workshop open to all genres: novels, poetry, children's books, creative nonfiction, and memoirs. Because some material would inevitably be adult in nature, we established a rule that prospective members had to be eighteen or older to join.

Since the fall of 1995, the St. Charles Writers Group (SCWG) has met around squared-off tables at the library on the second and fourth Saturday of each month. The honeymoon was glorious, but the relationship occasionally needed counseling. I had to remind a few members to talk about the text (not its author), avoid pontificating, and focus on how the work succeeds or fails in reaching its intended audience. One or two got on a soapbox, critiqued in belligerent tones, related long personal anecdotes, or argued fine points of grammar. Eventually my constant correcting or the group's frustrated body language sent these folks on their way.

The original members vanished one by one due, I suppose, to our practice of addressing a manuscript's problems as well as its strengths. Anyone seeking a mother's adoration didn't stay long. We went from occasional scribblers to dedicated writers crafting revisions with just as much enthusiasm as we had when rollicking through rough drafts. Today we're middle-aged writers working as police detective, computer programmer, hypnotherapist, teacher, publisher, journalist, homemaker, and technical writer.

Over the past few years I felt like Kevin Costner in *Field of Dreams* watching uniformed players step out of the cornfield to take up their positions. The group evolved from writers needing guidance to a group of friends who gather on Saturday morning to talk about writing. Though hardly a support group, we joke about how needy we'd be without it. Hearing the good-natured teasing and tawdry one-liners, I'd say the group today is as unified as a baseball mitt. Without a word from me they created and keep current a Web site; chat and network via e-mail; take turns writing updates (creative "minutes") of each meeting that are then e-mailed to everyone; meet for lunch after workshop; and organized Writers Anonymous, a weekly free-writing group. They even bring coffee and tea. And this year they conspired to play a joke on the group facilitator by including the word *quiche* in each manuscript turned in during one session, betting on whether I'd catch on.

The group grew. Today as many as thirty-five show up for winter meetings (the numbers decrease in summer). We lengthened the sessions to two and a half hours and limited submissions to seven space-and-a-half prose pages or three "average" poems (about thirty lines—or the equivalent in shorter or longer poems).

One benefit of having a large, diverse group is knowing I can defer to a computer junkie or professional essayist when I can't field a question about publishing on-line, or am ill-equipped to evaluate an article meant for *Cooking Light*. Instead of confounding the group, opening the workshop to a variety of genres stimulates and unites. When focusing on a poem, novelists are suitably self-deprecating ("I don't write poetry, but the punctuation in this stanza confuses me . . ."), while poets admit lack of expertise in, say, the detective thriller ("I usually don't read this kind of novel, but this character needs to be better motivated . . .").

At a typical session, members turn in new manuscripts for the group to critique before our next meeting, at which time they will be discussed. Each member is responsible for making copies of his own work for the other members of the group.

The session begins with announcements (publishing achievements, local readings, and so on), thirty-second introductions by prospective members, and brainstorming writing topics for next quarter.

We then spend thirty to sixty minutes on that day's topic. Lecturing only if the subject is arcane, I ordinarily provide a few insights, then promote give-and-take on issues as diverse as journaling, publishing, creative nonfiction, writer's block, structure in fiction, our favorite obscure writers, or a book discussion (we just did Rilke's *Letters to a Young Poet*). Occasionally we'll do freewriting on ideas generated by the group; for one session everyone brought in a different object (plastic snow brick maker, necklace—anything) on which we wrote five minutes, then read our jottings aloud. Freewriting also gets integrated with topic discussions when we cover imagery, writing from memory, and so forth.

Next comes the reading from the group novel. Two years ago we voted on members' one-page plot outlines, and now volunteers write successive chapters. If a member has finished his or her contribution (about 2,000 words), he'll read it to us.

With about an hour and a half remaining, we start on the manuscripts. Discussion averages about ten minutes per manuscript; we take less time for shorter or less needy work, more for longer or problematic tomes. The author may not talk during commentary; knowing his intentions might influence our response. Even with large numbers, this group's not shy, so I far from dominate discussion. After we finish, the author may briefly ask questions or offer explanations, and then we pass our edited manuscripts to him.

The last session of every quarter we have a group reading. The public's invited, but mostly it's a spouse or other family member who shows up. Members are encouraged, but not compelled, to read for about five minutes (again, due to large numbers) from present or past work.

In the best of groups, which I believe ours is, the facilitator and group have a great marriage. They regard each other with compassion and respect; go out together, but do their best work alone; disagree, but learn the other may have a point. Each wants to make the other laugh, arouse his sympathy, support his persona, guide him when lost, and accept his many flaws— my most prominent being an inveterate inattention to detail.

But yes, I did catch the quiche.

Members' Comments

Joselle D. Kehoe: One of the ways the group has helped me is receiving me as a writer. I've had work buddies, workout buddies, even math buddies, but never writing buddies. Someone not trying to find his place in the literary world would never notice so small an unfulfilled need. The difference is remarkable. It gave writing the priority I wanted to give it. The group gives me deadlines, an audience—and takes seriously the obligation I feel to write.

Frank Sobocienski (An anthology of criticism by sixteen members on a recent submission): Interesting surreal moment! Try saying that three times. Who they? O. sexist! Interesting analogy. Foreskin. I'm not sure what this needs, more sentences, less phrases . . . too clippy. My usual comments apply—GREAT WRITING STYLE. Punctuation & spelling need attention. Confusing. Tighten. The whole thing reads like a Tom Wolfe piece—kaleidoscopic. Wordy and tedious. You have a way with exaggeration! Doesn't your computer have spell check? Methuselah . . . one L . . . is oldest man in the world. Do you mean Medusa . . . woman with snakes on her to which Warhol subjected his Frankenstein? Repetitive. Excellent language . . . but with fewer words, fewer similes, metaphors, etc. Hospitals are great aren't they? The allusions were fun. Oh, me brother! Very awkward. Enjoyed this, Thank you.

Frank adds, "To think I drive thirty-five miles from Barrington to St. Charles every other Saturday for this kind of feedback. Too bad we don't meet more often!"

Nancy Wedemeyer: Writers string nouns and verbs like jewelers place pearls on necklaces, then add adjectives and prepositions, accent, and enhance. Writing is a solitary occupation. However, even singular creatures seek the camaraderie of fellows in their trade. As jewelers create guilds, writers form groups that function as a forum for their art and an arena to develop their skills. This is why I continue to be a part of the group, a treasure chest filled with precious gems. I am drawn to them like Tiffany to gold.

Susan Kraykowski (Relocated to Pennsylvania with her husband, but continues to critique manuscripts and e-mail us): I miss all of you. I miss your laughter, support, and needling—and the way I used to wake up on the second and fourth Saturdays of every month, "Oh boy! It's going to be a wonderful day!" I miss when we fall out along gender lines on some point, and shrug and say, "Oh, well, it's reaching half the audience anyway." I miss the aliases in updates and applauding when Dean isn't more than ten minutes late. I miss group novels, breast jokes, limericks, chapters out of sequence, puns, dead metaphors, new metaphors that become dead metaphors . . .

If I hadn't had this solid platform I wouldn't have leapt . . . even if I can't yet see the net.

Favorite Resources

BOOKS

Burroway, Janet. *Writing Fiction: A Guide to Narrative Craft.* New York: Longman, 2000.

Fussell, Paul, Jr. *Poetic Meter and Poetic Form.* New York: Random House, 1965.

Lamott, Anne. *Bird by Bird: Some Instructions on Writing and Life*. New York: Anchor Books, 1995.

Lodge, David. *The Art of Fiction*. New York: Viking, 1992.

Padgett, Rod, editor. *Handbook of Poetic Forms*. New York: Teachers & Writers Collaborative, 1987.

Sims, Norman, editor. *The Literary Journalists*. New York: Ballantine Books, 1984.

> **No one can write a best seller by trying to. He must write with complete sincerity; the clichés that make you laugh, the hackneyed characters, the well-worn situations, the commonplace story that excites your derision, seem neither hackneyed, well worn, nor commonplace to him.**
> —W. SOMERSET MAUGHAM

An Agent Among Us

Literary Agents and Writing Groups

JENNIE DUNHAM, DUNHAM LITERARY, INC.

~

WRITING GROUP NAME: She visits many!

WRITING GROUP LOCATION: New York and anywhere writers gather (a regularly featured speaker at writing conferences)

TYPE OF WRITERS: This essay applies to all writers!

WRITING GROUPS support individual writers by giving them a place to discuss the art of creating. So let me just say from the beginning that I come from the enemy camp. Or at least it can seem that way. I'm a literary agent.

As such it's my job to talk about marketing. Sometimes I have to deliver bad news. "No, they decided not to make an offer for the manuscript after all." It makes my day to deliver good news. "I have an offer for you!" But in general my job is to talk about a writer's business, and business is marketing, negotiating, and writing checks.

Writers, you will not be surprised to hear, want to sell their books. They want to receive money and recognition for their labors, and they want people to read their books. And they are working harder than ever to have polished manuscripts because an editor may like the voice and story but not want to pay money for a book that needs substantial work.

The more polished a manuscript I get, the less editorial commenting I need to do, which means I can go straight to selling the manuscript. I'm more likely to take on a client whose work is polished, and the chance of a sale is higher. Writing groups help make manuscripts more polished, and so it comes as no surprise that I like writing groups because I find that many good writers and manuscripts come from them.

This is where, I think, writing groups are more popular and useful than ever. The more people who give careful, considered feedback about a manuscript, the better. It certainly helps if the people who give the feedback are good readers. If they can analyze a story and describe what works and doesn't work, the writer receiving the critique has found gold. Not everyone gives good critiques, but for those who do, it is a gift. And those in writing groups tend to be better on the whole at giving these critiques than the average person on the street because everyone in a writing group deals with similar issues and practices giving critiques regularly.

And to be blunt, it's my job to sell the manuscript, not write or edit it.

Agenting, however, is changing. Fewer and fewer editors have time to edit, which means that they want to buy manuscripts that are practically perfect already. And that means that agents are giving more and more editorial advice in order to sell books. Because of this, I end up talking about the dramatic arc of stories and whether or not the characters are believable. And more than talking about these, I need to come up with suggestions so that the author can fix any parts that might keep the book from selling.

We can midwife by making suggestions about the story, but we can't do the writer's job for him or her, so we tend to focus on what we *can* do: the marketing. We're trying to give you the tools to lift you up and let your work shine. We're trying to help you reach the audience that will enjoy your books.

One day I received a manuscript from a writer I'd been representing for a short time. Her characters were believable and had real, human dilemmas to face and resolve. One of her weaknesses, however, was creating a satisfying arc of the story. The chapters tended to be episodic, several of the loose ends weren't tied up by the end, and the climax didn't feel, well, as climactic as it should. It's not unusual for a writer to have read and reread passages so often that it's hard for him or her to see the big picture, so I read the manuscript carefully, and I made some suggestions about the parts of the novel I felt needed improvement before I could submit it to editors. She listened attentively and told me she'd get back to me.

I expected her to call in a few days and tell me she understood what I was saying and why, and that she would need some time to revise the manuscript. I was surprised, however, when she called in a few days to say, "My writing group doesn't agree with you." It was as if I'd attacked her personally, which was not my intention at all. Several members of her writing group were hugely successful, and they told her to stick up for herself and her story. She thought it was marketable as it was, and she didn't want to change it.

Let me say here that writers shouldn't compromise the artistry of what they've written. But if changes don't weaken the artistry and do make the manuscript more saleable, it behooves a writer to address the constructive criticism from the agent (or editor). The point is to make the best manuscript possible so that the agent can get the highest advance possible, so that reviewers will praise it, and ultimately so that readers will buy, enjoy, and recommend the book.

Writing groups are not on the front lines of marketing, at least not in the same way an agent is. An author may have experience with a couple of publishers or even a handful. And many authors hear gossip. But an agent spends each day keeping in touch with editors about what they are publishing, what books are selling well, and what editors are looking to buy.

This writer gave me an ultimatum: submit the novel to several publishers or she would find another agent. On the strength of the writing I decided to try a few publishers. I submitted the novel to five editors. All of them declined to make an offer, and one or two of them even cited the same concerns that I had. In the end the writer and I parted ways amicably, and as far as I know she has not sold her novel.

One time a client whose writing is gorgeous sent me a manuscript. I said it was fine except that the ending didn't fit at all. She didn't know what to do to fix it. Several times she put the story in a drawer while she worked on other pieces hoping that while she was working with her conscious mind on something else, her subconscious would percolate so she could fix it when she brought it out again. But that didn't work. She took it to her writing group and discussed it. Several people had ideas for what to do. She considered a happy ending, a sad ending, a compromise ending, a funny ending, an ambiguous ending. But none of these felt right to my client. Still, it was this conversation that invigorated her thinking about the ending enough that when she went back to her desk at home, she came up with the perfect ending. She had a reversal of circumstances and characters at the end that was heartwarming, funny, and satisfying all at the same time. It worked. And most of the reviews mentioned the ending, which had stumped her for so long. In this case it was the group process that made all the difference.

Over the years I've visited a fair number of writing groups. It's always fun and interesting to see the group rally behind a writer who is working out the kinks of character, voice, and plot. And sometimes, although rarely, I make a connection with a writer that works for us both. On one visit, I heard part of a story read aloud. Six months later I couldn't get the story out of my mind, and I sent an e-mail to a person in the group I knew to inquire about that writer and her memorable story. When I reached the writer she explained that she didn't have an agent. She considered my inquiry and later replied that she would like to have me represent her. I sent her my agency contract, she signed it, and I submitted her manuscript to one editor on an exclusive basis because I thought this story might be a good match. Three weeks later I got a call from that editor with an offer for the manuscript. In just that short time, the writer's life changed. She went from unpublished to published status, and for the first time she was in a position to receive money for her writing.

~

In short, while there can be prickly situations between writing groups and agents, I believe that great things can come from writing groups. I recommend that most writers join them. A writing group can give invaluable help with constructive criticism and can provide the catalyst to make a manuscript jump from good to great. Beyond that, a writing group can be a warm, supportive group of friends helping each other during tough times and cheering for each other in good times.

PART II

ORGANIZING AND MAINTAINING A WRITING GROUP

■

> We are a species that needs and wants to understand who we are. Sheep lice do not seem to share this longing, which is one reason why they write so little.
>
> —ANNE LAMOTT, novelist

Whatever the structure of your writing group, sharing opportunities, acknowledging others' accomplishments, and motivating members beyond rejection are important to the community of a group. But the heart of a good writing group lies in the ability of members to give and receive constructive critiques. Some of these essays will help you learn this delicate art form. Other essays offer insights into maintaining a productive group.

What to Pack for Your First Writing Group Meeting

Karen Lewis

~

WRITING GROUP NAME: DCW (only members know its meaning)
WRITING GROUP LOCATION: Amherst, New York
TYPE OF WRITERS: Poets, essayists, and short story writers

To make any trip successful it helps to know what to pack. How many times have you traveled only to wish you had brought those shoes or that book?! I'm going to show you what to include in your writer's bag, so that you can ease into a new group experience with confidence, so that you don't arrive feeling unprepared.

Depending on where you live, you will likely need to bring some sort of overcoat or sweater to ward off any potential chill you may experience during your journey. In a group setting, *honesty* can function as an overcoat. The task of the group is to deliver skilled, comprehensive critique when a piece of writing is presented for review. Every member needs to understand that you are working together to serve the word. If you feel the need to sugarcoat your opinion, or you worry that your own work will meet with social judgment, then you are going to feel like running for your overcoat and heading out the door. Productive groups understand that opinion, in this setting, is solicited—it is what drives the group. All members should feel free to give honest comments. The key is to keep your remarks focused on the writing, not the writer.

The clean-underwear rule your mother hopefully taught you is integral to your feeling prepared. It helps you to relax if you feel that the core of your sense of self is protected. It affirms your *integrity*. This quality especially comes into play in the area of protecting others' creative ideas. One should not have to spend time worrying about plagiarism, or the stealing of thought. All work being handled within the group should be considered private property. Do not share it unless you have the permission of the author. Work being addressed by the group is usually unpublished and all rights to that work should be respected. You wouldn't want other people to tell tales about the kind of undergarments you wear to meetings, so treat your fellow members' work with the same delicacy. Your honor and the group's reliability depend on it.

Include a handy, portable umbrella . . . just in case it rains. There are times within the life of a group when sensitive issues are discussed, which may or may not necessitate the sharing of tears. Often people write about beloved subjects. It is imperative that group members keep conversation *confidential*. Sharing can help develop intimate group dynamics; however, everyone must first agree to keep this kind of communication private. Remembering to pack an umbrella is a reassuring safeguard designed to respect and protect all members.

Add an empty bag. You never know what you're going to want to bring home. Don't leave something wonderful behind just because you didn't have room for it in your case. Be *open-minded* and receptive to the surprises in store for you. Fill your bag with generosity and tolerance. You will find that your creativity will soar in response and that the group experience will be joyful as well as constructive. Once trust is established you will find that *sharing* comes naturally. It is likely you'll be leaving future meetings with yet another book to read, submission suggestions, or tokens of appreciation. Best of all are those meetings that leave your mind filled with new ideas or inspiration.

Include fun stuff—funky earrings or colorful pens—anything that marks you as an intriguing person to be around. It will feed the creative collective. Whatever you do, make sure to walk in the door with your *sense of humor* intact. The best groups, the ones that get the job done in a reasonable amount of time, love to laugh. Incorporate, into the structure of your group life, ways to maximize the good feelings inherent in the pleasure of each other's company.

Last, but most important, when you are on your way to your first group meeting, excited about the opportunity yet a little nervous about making a commitment to a group that has yet to gel, it is important to remember that the other writers are probably feeling the same way. When you get to the home, restaurant, library, or wherever you've agreed to meet, it is essential that you consciously leave one very important element behind. Park your *ego* with the car! A strong sense of self-esteem can be a beautiful thing to behold; however, too much self-centeredness has a negative effect within groups. Remember, you are joining a group; a collective of individuals, a society of sorts, and it is crucial to enter into this relationship with a firm grasp on any tendency toward egocentrism. You don't want to leave the impression that you've packed for an *ego*-trip; better to think of it as a cruise, where you all sleep in similar-size cabins.

So there you are, standing in the doorway. Keep in mind the reasons that you are here—to serve the word so that you can become a better writer and to enjoy the company of other writers. Open yourself to the experience, take a deep breath, and walk right on in.

Favorite Resources

AUDIO

McKee, Robert. *Story: Substance, Structure, Style and the Principles of Screenwriting*. New York: Harper Audio, 1997. This audio is available in book form as well. Additionally, McKee leads a very successful seminar based on the book at many locations throughout the world. (I've taken one of his New York City seminars.) For more information on Robert McKee's Story Seminar, contact: Two Arts, Inc., P.O. Box 452930, Los Angeles, CA 90045; phone (888) 676-2533 or fax (310) 645-6928; Web site: www.mckeestory.com.

BOOKS

Ackerman, Diane. *A Natural History of the Senses*. New York: Vintage Books, 1991.

Gass, William H. *Reading Rilke: Reflections on the Problems of Translation*. New York: Alfred Knopf, 1999.

Hirshfield, Jane. *Nine Gates: Entering the Mind of Poetry*. New York: Harper Perennial, 1997.

King, Stephen. *On Writing: A Memoir of the Craft*. New York: Scribner, 2000.

Woolridge, Susan Goldsmith. *poem crazy: freeing your life with words*. New York: Three Rivers Press, 1996.

RETREAT

The International Women's Writing Guild offers a weeklong summer conference and weekend retreat called "Remember the Magic." For information, contact: Hannalore Hahn, P.O. Box 810, Gracie Station, New York, NY 10028; e-mail: iwwg@iwwg.com; Web site: www.iwwg.com/index.html.

> **For a creative writer possession of the truth is less important than emotional sincerity.**
> —GEORGE ORWELL

Welcome to the Writing Life
On the Value of Writing Groups

Carol LaChapelle

~

WRITING GROUP NAME: Writing group facilitator
WRITING GROUP LOCATION: Chicago, Illinois
TYPE OF WRITERS: Memoir, nature, and essay writers

It's six p.m. on a warm summer Friday in Chicago. I'm sitting alone in a coffeehouse writing. I've spent a little over an hour and have managed almost two hundred pretty usable words for an op-ed piece I'm submitting to the *New York Times*. Two hundred words, not quite one full page, two hundred words on the way to a six hundred–word essay that no one's asked me to write, or is waiting for, or may even publish.

I've agonized over every one of those two hundred words, rewriting, rereading, scratching out, scribbling in the margins, running my hands repeatedly through my hair, taking another drink of seltzer, asking the nice young man behind the counter—again—to please lower the volume on the bass-driven CD now thumping through the room, the floor, my skull.

Ah, the writing life: Glamour! Romance! Fame!

~

I first started teaching writing in 1986, when I was a graduate student at the University of Illinois. Freshman comp, two to three classes of twenty or so eighteen-year-olds, most of them uninterested in writing, in reading, or working at either. I endured that purgatory for several years, then struck out on my own, changing venues, changing students. Now I teach mostly adults, at places like the Newberry Library and the Ragdale Foundation (an artist's retreat), both workshops in memoir writing and nature writing.

The people who show up in these workshops are a varied lot—some men but mostly women, all ages, from all professions and none, and all with an itch to write. They've come to me to help them scratch it.

I typically begin the first session of a workshop series with the unerring wisdom of writer Gene Fowler: "Writing is easy, all you do is stare at a blank sheet of paper 'til drops of blood form on your forehead." It sets a kind of tone. Besides, I like to get the truth out on the table from the start. OK, I continue, you're going to have fun in this workshop, you'll learn some useful things about writing, you'll meet some nice like-minded people, but, most important, you'll suffer. Like all writers who have to turn white space into words that engage and please a reader, you'll experience equal parts dread, satisfaction, despair, and elation.

Welcome to the writing life!

I find that most people are relieved to hear my little speech. It resonates; most of us think we're the only ones who have to write a lot of crap before finding a passable paragraph or two. It's comforting to know that this *is* the process. It's writing. As a writer, you've got to figure out how to get that great idea or image or story out of your head and down onto three or five or ten double-spaced, typed pages that someone other than your doting mother or loving spouse wants to read.

And that is not easy. And it's why people show up at a workshop: to have a reason to work so hard—*especially when they don't have to.*

The heart of any writing workshop—its raison d'etre—is the workshop part, when people volunteer to have the group read and respond to their drafts. If it's done right, everyone is putting a lot of effort into the process. The writer has presented a draft that's already been revised three or four times, is neither too long nor too short, and that needs no lengthy introduction. The readers have to do a slow, close reading of the draft, looking beyond the words for structure, sequence, coherence. (Donald Murray, a New England writer and writing teacher, says, "Writing isn't magic, but then magic isn't magic either." When writers read, they look for the chains and pulleys behind the curtain.)

In my workshops, I always read the writer's draft aloud to the group, then we take a few minutes for everyone—including the writer—to write specific comments and suggestions onto their copies. Then the discussion begins.

Because each of us knows how damn nerve-racking it is to put our best effort out there only to find out that, oops, not quite, we are always kind to the writer. We don't lie, we don't hedge, we tell the truth, but we are kind.

And our kindness shows up mostly in how seriously we have read the work and how specifically we will talk about it. Here's what works, we tell the writer: The introduction brings us right into the story; the pacing is great; good, strong verbs. Here's what needs work, we tell the writer: The dialogue feels stilted; we need a bit more description on page 4; maybe that third paragraph is really the second.

The writer then gets to speak—for the first time since we began. To ask any specific questions of us: Did you find the brother likeable? Does it need a stronger ending? We give our answers and say why.

And then we end the discussion, profusely thanking the writer for having done the hard work of preparing a good draft for us to talk about, to learn from, to be inspired by when we all next sit down at our journals, legal pads, or computers.

Then it's time for the next draft, and it begins again: The shuffle of papers being distributed around the table, the lingering conversation from the last discussion, the sigh of relief from the first writer, the nervous laughter of the next.

And so each week goes, until we reach the last. By this time, if all goes well, a disparate collection of people, personalities, talent, and industry has melded itself into a writing group. In the process, they've learned a bit more about writing, about reading, and about the extent of their devotion to the writing life.

And if someone leaves the workshop knowing that she does not want to do the work required to call herself a writer, she has learned a great deal. And those who become or remain committed to the work are encouraged to join another workshop or writing group *immediately* or to form their own. And by now they know why: without readers waiting for their countless revisions—critical, serious readers—most of them will not stare at that blank sheet of paper long and regularly enough.

"Writers don't so much finish a piece," I once read, "as abandon it." Yes, I could have rewritten the op-ed piece for at least another few weeks. But luckily I grew bored with it and finally sent it off. But not before reading it to my own writing group. Some of the suggestions were right on; some missed the mark. Typical. On the final revision, I chose which ones to take seriously, and which to disregard. After all, I am the author, i.e., the authority, of the piece. The buck does stop here. It's both a comforting and unsettling thought.

Welcome to the writing life.

Favorite Resources

BOOKS

Lamott, Anne. *Bird by Bird: Some Instructions on Writing and Life*. New York: Anchor Books, 1995.

Zinsser, William. *On Writing Well: The Classic Guide to Writing Nonfiction*. New York: Harper Resource, 2001.

WEB SITE

www.carollachapelle.com

> **The difference between the almost right word and the right word is really a large matter—it's the difference between the lightning bug and the lightning.**
> —MARK TWAIN

On-Line and in Touch

Organizing a Writing Group in Cyberspace

Mary Pat Mahoney

~

WRITING GROUP NAME: The Busy Bees & The Busy Middles
WRITING GROUP LOCATION: Colleyville, Texas
TYPE OF WRITERS: Children's writers

I N A PERFECT WORLD, I sit down at my computer and write from eight A.M. to five P.M., finish in time for a home-cooked gourmet meal with my family, and afterward leisurely revise my latest manuscript or catch up on reading.

In the real world, I put in eight hours on the job, ferry my sons to after-school activities, prepare dinner, and attempt to make a dent in the pile of laundry. When the house is finally quiet, I can usually squeeze in two hours of writing, if I don't fall asleep first! There's barely enough time to write, let alone get together with my fellow writers for a critique session.

That's why I was so excited to start an on-line writing group. This has proven to be an ideal way to connect with other writers without adding yet another meeting away from home. The group offers nearly everything an in-the-flesh group offers: feedback on my writing, information about new markets, a forum for ideas, and the opportunity to make new friends. Best of all, I can be a part of my writing group when my schedule allows—even if that means midnight!

Getting Started

The first step to getting your group started is to find like-minded writers. You may already know one or two who want to start a group. If you don't, consider joining an organization like Mystery Writers of American or the Society for Children's Book Writers and Illustrators. Talk to your librarian; he or she may know writers you can contact. Check the newspaper. Some papers publish a calendar that lists meetings of various organizations; a writing group may be among them. If you join an existing group, be sure to express your interest in forming an on-line group. You might be surprised at the interest, especially if you volunteer to be the facilitator.

It might be even easier to start your on-line group on-line! An Internet search for writing groups will turn up all kinds of sites. Yahoo!Groups (www.yahoogroups.com) will allow you to start a new group for free or join an existing one.

My group started with seven people. It has grown and shrunk since the beginning, but seems to feel just right with eight members. Don't be surprised if people drop out or aren't as active as you'd like them to be. Even though writers come and go, you will eventually develop a core of dedicated members whom you trust.

How many people should you start with? Like an in-the-flesh group, the more participants the more comments you'll get on your writing. But more participants also means you'll have more manuscripts in your in-box. Decide how much time you want to devote to reading and responding to e-mail and how much feedback you want on your writing.

The hardest part of getting an on-line group going is finding writers who want to commit to a group. The word *commit* is operative here! If one person is writing as a hobby and another has serious ambitions, group members may be frustrated or the group may fall apart. Try to find motivated, energetic writers who share your goals. If you want to get published, they should too.

How an On-Line Group Works

1. Send a manuscript within the body of an e-mail to all the members of the group.

2. Create a standard for the subject line so members can easily identify mail. For example, *WriteNow: ms/Three Pigs* means the writing group called Write Now is receiving a manuscript titled "Three Pigs."

3. Use another standard for the subject line when sending back critiques. For example, *WriteNow: cr/Three Pigs* means the mail contains a critique of "Three Pigs."

4. Agree to a time period for members to read and critique manuscripts. If your group is reading short children's stories, a week is reasonable. If you're reading adult novel chapters, you may need more time.

5. Write your critique in all caps. Your comments will stand out in the text, and the writer won't miss any suggestions.

6. Consider using the sandwich-style critique: say something nice at the start, comment on the text, and conclude with positive remarks.

7. Use the "Reply All" feature so all members of the group can benefit from the critiques.

The Top Ten On-Line Tips

Before you start your group, consider these tips for success.

1. **Have a leader.** Like any other organization, if no one is in charge, the group will dissolve. Once the group is up and running, there isn't much work for a leader to do. He or she will need to keep a current list of e-mail addresses, have a copy of the group's guidelines for new members, and help resolve any conflicts that arise. The leader can also be chief cheerleader/motivator by setting group goals such as challenging members to enter contests or use writing prompts.

2. **Keep it simple.** Guidelines for the group should be straightforward and easy to remember. Don't make the rules so involved that members spend more time critiquing than working on their own writing projects.

3. **Stay flexible.** Allow the rules to change and evolve. Our group started with the stipulation that members would submit a manuscript at least once a month. When that didn't happen, we dropped the rule rather than lose members.

4. **Avoid the red pencil syndrome!** Encourage members to focus on the big picture (plot, character, setting, and so

forth) rather than spelling and grammar errors. Most of us can correct those on our own.

5. **Decide when to read.** Should you read someone else's critique of a manuscript before you write your own? Members who are insecure about their critiquing skills will find it helpful to read someone else's comments first. However, if your group decides to do this, avoid the temptation of critiquing the critique! Keep the focus on the manuscript. When members write their own critiques before reading those of the rest of the group, comments are varied and fresh. Frequently, several members will point out the same weak spot.

6. **Reread before hitting the send button.** What may be obvious to you as a joke or humorous remark may not be obvious to the receiver of your e-mail. Emoticons (those little smiley faces) or a parenthetical "ha-ha" can help.

7. **Share successes, rejections, and market information.** You'll build group trust and support if members look out for each other.

8. **Develop a thick skin.** Whether it's on-line or in-the-flesh, you can't take criticism personally. Your job isn't to defend your work; it's to improve it. Treat critiques the way you treat suggestions your mother-in-law makes: use the ones you like and ignore the rest. If several people in your group make the same suggestion or see the same problem, consider their opinions seriously.

9. **Keep the lines of communication open.** If you are going out of town, need a break from writing, will be changing

your e-mail address, or encounter something else that will prevent you from responding in a timely fashion, let the members of the group know. There is nothing worse than sending out a manuscript and not hearing back from the group.

10. **Be on-line!** It sounds obvious, but we all know people who have e-mail and never check it. Be sure members are committed to reading and responding to manuscripts.

With time and trust, you can create a group that works well together. And, while none of us may ever have a perfect writing life, a nearly perfect writing group is within our grasp.

Favorite Resources

BOOKS

Geisel, Theodore (Dr. Seuss). *Oh the Places You'll Go*. New York: Random House, 1990.

Hacker, Diana. *A Writer's Reference*. Boston: Bedford, 1992.

Juster, Norton. *The Phantom Tollbooth*. New York: Random House, 1989.

King, Stephen. *On Writing: A Memoir of the Craft*. New York: Pocket, 2001.

Seuling, Barbara. *How to Write a Children's Book and Get It Published*. New York: Macmillan, 1991.

Society of Children's Book Writers and Illustrators. *From Typewriter to Printed Page . . . Facts You Need to Know.* Beverly Hills, CA: Society of Children's Book Writers and Illustrators, 1999.

Strunk, William, and E. B. White. *The Elements of Style.* Boston, MA: Allyn & Bacon, 2000.

Wyndham, Lee. *Writing for Children and Teenagers.* Cincinnati: Writer's Digest, 1989.

WEB SITE

www.newwritersmarket.com

> **Writers aren't exactly people . . . they're a whole lot of people trying to be one person.**
> —F. SCOTT FITZGERALD

Giving Good Group
Critiques That Help

RAQUELLE AZRAN

~

WRITING GROUP NAME: The Writers' Circle
WRITING GROUP LOCATION: Tel Aviv, Israel
TYPE OF WRITERS: Fiction and nonfiction novelists, essayists, and memoirists

I'VE BEEN WRITING ever since I can remember. The world has always seemed less threatening, and people easier to relate to, with paper and pencil at hand. I began writing in earnest when I bought my first computer ten years ago, setting aside time from family and work for sweaty sessions at the keyboard. Writing for me, then, was an incredibly private activity, not to be shared and never to be shown. With time, and especially after participating in two writing workshops, I discovered the critical importance of reader-writer interaction. I knew that for my writing to take off, I'd need feedback. I couldn't do it alone.

And then one day, about two years ago, I saw an ad in the local paper: *Writing group looking for new members. For details, call* _____. I called and found myself one Monday evening sitting in a living room with ten popcorn-munching strangers, all listening attentively to work being read aloud. The meeting was casual but focused, with no official leader. They were a mixed bunch of ten Americans and South Africans, who'd been meeting every other Monday evening for more than five years to share their writing. The pediatrician wrote tongue-in-cheek murder mysteries. The pilot was struggling with his memoirs and the physiotherapist was in the middle of a historical novel. Several group members had already been published. I brought a short piece of mine along, thinking that if I felt comfortable enough, and if the group seemed professional, I'd welcome their comments. I did, and they were, and I joined.

This is our writing group procedure: Three people volunteer to read for each meeting. The week before, they e-mail their work to the group, to enable us to respond and the writer to consider our comments. At the meeting, each writer brings copies of the revised work to hand out, and reads the work aloud. We then critique the work, break for coffee, and continue with the next writer.

~

It was my turn to read for the next meeting. Although I usually write creative nonfiction, I found myself at the keyboard, grinding out a piece of erotic fiction about a lesbian encounter in the shower room of a gym. I called the story "Body Work."

> The only way I could afford to join the new gym was by working there three afternoons a week. So from two until seven P.M., I answered the phones and handed out clean towels. The minute my shift was over, I'd head for the locker room, change into my workout gear, and hit the machines. Thirty minutes

pounding the treadmill, another thirty on the stepper, one hour pumping iron and grinding away on the fitness equipment.

Yesterday, I pushed myself even harder than usual. Slick with sweat, muscles quivering, I ignored the admiring glances of the woman working out next to me and concentrated on my breathing. In, push, out. In, push, out.

"You're really good," she said. "I've been watching you for awhile. I like the way you use your body."

"Thanks." I sneaked a quick glance. I'd seen her around the gym before. Medium height, spiky black hair, olive skin, now beaded with sweat. Some good jewelry. A classy professional, maybe a lawyer. I caught faint traces of her musky perfume.

"I'm Karen."

"Hi," I said and added another ten pounds to the counter-weight. When I push myself to the maximum, closing my eyes helps me concentrate. She got the hint and backed off. I silently counted down the last set. Workout over, I grabbed my towel and went off to shower.

It was a slow day and I had the shower room all to myself. I quickly stripped and turned on the water taps to maximum. Nothing in the world beats feeling your muscles gently uncurl while standing under a stinging hot shower. I stretched up into the heat, all five feet eight inches of me, purring with pleasure. The water streamed down my face and body and swirled around my toes. Through the steam, I could see my skin turning rosy and my nipples soft and full.

I e-mailed the story to the group and waited for feedback. I didn't have long to wait. "Well done," wrote Z (after taking a cold shower). "A fine-fingered job, but the ending requires more penetrating subtlety." "A very sensual story with a great ending, but add more description about her skin, her magnificent breasts . . ." suggested L. "I think you have a problem with logistics," commented O., pointing out a series of positions that he found improbable. R. supplied technical data. "Hands in water that long wouldn't be velvety, they'd be pruny. Now if she had soap or shampoo on her hands . . ." Even reserved E. opined that this was "a pretty hot piece."

Three readers hit the nail on the head. They pointed out that by opting for a bodies-only approach, I'd lost my audience. Wrote B., "You've written about people I'd like to know more about. If it's just erotica, who cares?" G. chimed in with "your character loses her voice right after the beginning." And M. left no doubt about his reaction. "It is undoubtedly a highly explicit and competent erotic work, but by dehumanizing it, you killed my interest."

So I went back to my story, and gave Gail, my protagonist in the shower, a voice.

My awakening body stirred memories I thought I'd managed to forget. Sid, you bastard, I cursed silently. We were so good together. During the day, I waited impatiently to finish work so I could return to the wildness of our bodies. Then one day I came home and found you packing. It's over, baby, you said, leaving me wet with passion, wet with tears.

A velvety hand glided across my stomach. My eyes shot open. "I told you I like the way you use your body," she said. I froze, shocked both by my recklessness and by desire. Karen stood facing me, her generous mouth smiling. Olive breasts, dark nippled, curved into a small waist. Her flat stomach and taut thighs mirrored my own. Rising up on scarlet tipped toes, she gently kissed me on the lips and waited.

> I sighed, unwilling to decide. My mind demanded familiar
> male hardness yet my body whispered its sudden desire for the
> moist softness of a woman.

I rewrote and revised and printed copies to hand out, still
not sure whether the story worked. I did know that writing
it had been unusually difficult. Deciding how explicitly to
write and using language I'd never before set down on paper
had felt like tiptoeing through a minefield of explosive four-
letter words.

The meeting began. One of the three scheduled readers was
a no-show, so my piece was allotted two full hours for discussion. And what a discussion! Depending on the piece and
author, our group critiques in one of two ways: either a general
analysis, or line-by-line editing. In this case, it was a free for all.
Feedback ranged from A[ghast] to Z[at's the way to go], with
people bringing in their own personal histories to justify their
comments: "I would never have reacted that way" and "I don't
believe that any woman would have dared to _____" and
"The eroticism, for me, centered upon _____." Everyone,
including normally reticent members, felt involved enough to
express their views on the topic, the writing, the genre. Their
comments were wide-ranging, perspicacious, and fair. The
group commented that this was one of the best meetings ever. I
emerged from the meeting more convinced than ever of the
value of a good writing group.

~

Writing is always risk-taking. You put yourself, and your
words, on the line, not knowing whether the piece works. A

good writing group will point out what doesn't work without imposing opinions or destroying you in the process. They'll tell you what does work, and share your pride and sense of accomplishment. If you are fortunate enough to be, as I am, in a writing group where mutual trust and professionalism coexist, then you have granted yourself the best wish that any genie could possibly grant a fisherman.

Favorite Resources

BOOKS

Lamott, Ann. *Bird by Bird: Some Instructions on Writing and Life.* New York: Anchor Books, 1995.

Lerner, Betsy. *The Forest for the Trees.* New York: Riverhead Books, 2000.

"Writers on Writing." *New York Times* 2000–2001 series.

SUPERB EXAMPLES OF WRITING

Butler, Robert Olen.
Some short stories, such as one in which he writes in the voice of a young Vietnamese woman or a Vietnamese soldier, are uncanny.

Fadiman, Anne. *Ex Libris: Confessions of a Common Reader.* New York: Farrar Straus and Giroux, 1998.

Michaels, Anne. *Fugitive Pieces.* New York: Random House, 1996. This was a New York Times Notable Book, winner of the Lannan Fiction and Guardian Fiction awards.

O'Connor, Flannery. *Everything That Rises Must Converge*. New York: Farrar Straus and Giroux, 1956.
Or any collection of O'Connor's short stories.

LITERARY PUBLICATIONS

Granta: The Magazine of New Writing (Great Britain)

The Iowa Review (United States)

WEB SITES

www.pw.org
Poets & Writers magazine on-line

www.writersdigest.com
Writer's Digest on-line

And for digging down deep, nothing beats an intensive writing workshop.

> . . . no writing is a waste of time, . . . no creative work where the feelings, the imagination, the intelligence must work.
> —BRENDA UELAND

Six Voices

The Story of a Poets' Group

RASMA HAIDRI

~

WRITING GROUP NAME: The Poets

WRITING GROUP LOCATION: Wisconsin. Haidri currently resides in Bodo, Norway.

TYPE OF WRITERS: Poets

IN 1999 I LEFT MY JOB, friends, and relatives in Wisconsin and moved to Hawaii to write. Of all the ties I severed, it was my writing group I missed most. We were six women who met biweekly in our homes to give each other feedback and encouragement. I called our group the Poets. Together we developed an instinct for language and a precision and honesty in writing that became so natural I no longer think about how my writing improved as a result. But the other day I was handed a piece of stark evidence. My daughter, writing a paper on AIDS, asked me if I knew how the HIV virus passed to humans. I scanned my brain for facts, and suddenly remembered I had written a poem on the subject. "Tampeeka and the Man" had been my clever rendering of the first HIV transmission when a tame but ominous pet monkey bit her master.

I looked for the poem, certain "Tampeeka" would impress my daughter. I finally found it, a single typed sheet filed under *T* in my cabinet. "Wow, it's old," she said as I handed her the crisp page. Her eyes went immediately to the green ink in the margin where I had recorded the Poets' comments.

"Let knowledge of disease be in reader, not in monkey . . ."

"Don't read that!" I interrupted, aware that my hidden motive in showing her the poem was to establish its merit. The Poets had slaughtered "Tampeeka" a decade earlier and I had shelved it away until a more enlightened audience would appreciate its innuendo. Now "Tampeeka" would get its due. I asked my daughter to read it aloud, so I could hear it again after all these years.

She started out fine, but soon her careful reading deteriorated into yelps of laughter. "*Whose* arm is it *now*—the monkey's or the man's? What does 'shudder of hot night air' *mean*?" When she came to my triumphant final line, "Waited for what would happen next," followed by the handwritten note "*baffles reader*" she put the poem down and announced, "They were right."

She went back to her report, and I picked up the poem. My eyes, too, went right to the comments. I recalled my dejection when the Poets had failed to embrace my masterpiece. But now I was struck by how mild their remarks had been—and how helpful.

"*Let monkey be more suspect from the start.*" OK, so they had been willing to let me have my premise but wanted it to be more convincing.

"*Read Bly's* News of the Universe." In other words, learn from the masters.

"Try it as a prose poem." Find a form to fit the material. In this case, by telling more I might have shown more. The Poets clearly stated their problems in reading the poem and gave specific suggestions for revision. All I remember feeling was their overwhelming disapproval. I heeded none of their advice and promptly forgot about the piece. After all, speculating about HIV was not a driving impulse. Writing poems was, though, and I stayed with the group.

In this early stage of my relationship with the Poets, I couldn't process feedback that I didn't immediately understand. I said I wanted help with revision, but as with "Tampeeka" all I heard was a thumbs-up-or-down judgment that made me give up on the poem or push it toward publication. Our group would not have flourished if we had looked to each other for simple approval or disapproval. Our commitment was to writing the best poems we could, and to this end we learned to sacrifice ego and its accompanying insecurities. We gave each other real support by focusing on the poems, not ourselves. We scrutinized each poem for authenticity and discrepancy. We spoke of "What the poem seems to want to say." I see now that the Poets' comments on "Tampeeka" pointed out the hints the poem gave about what needed to be expressed. It was I who stood in its way.

Of course, we didn't need to follow every bit of feedback. Each of us honed her ability to sift through the group's comments. A poet might follow every suggestion for one poem, and then ignore all comments on another one. The poem's actualization was not a group effort. I remember the time someone announced that one of her poems was coming out in *Poetry.* "I didn't make any of the changes you suggested!" she added.

As in most good relationships, intuition went into our beginnings. We met through common acquaintances, or familiarity with each other's writing. We had all shared poems with people, but we each longed for an effective writing group. After some serendipitous networking, the six of us were brought together by our mutual attraction to each other's writing and a common vision for a group. We decided to meet weekly and quickly developed shared leadership. We rotated houses and started each evening with conversation and coffee for about a half-hour. Then we looked at poems.

Our methodology was built on instinct and experience: the poet handed out copies of her poem, and while she read everyone else listened without comment and took notes. Then each of us responded to the poem while the poet listened without comment and took notes. Questions stated during feedback were understood to be rhetorical for the poet to answer within herself. Our no-interruption-during-feedback practice was integral. When the poet read to attentive listeners, she felt heard. When readers responded to an attentive, nondefensive poet, she felt heard. It was by listening that we became better writers, letting our poems reveal themselves to us during our sessions. We usually spent four hours together, looking at one poem from each of us, and no one left until we were done.

We avoided nondescriptive terms: "Good," "Bad," "Nice," "I liked it." Feedback was specific. "The energy of the poem picked up when. . . ." "I felt a shift in tone or language here. . . ." "This word made me. . . . I wondered if you meant. . . . Have you thought to. . . . This reminds me of. . . ." We told what drew our attention and what seemed not to belong. When the readers were finished responding, it was the poet's turn to talk. She did not explain or defend her poem but brought up the issues she had with it and asked for clarification of comments. "Did you mean. . . . What if I were to. . . . No one mentioned the line I thought was a problem. . . ." The poet did not need to address each comment or express her disagreement with any of them. She ended with, "Thank you; this was helpful." Even when the suggestions weren't followed, the poet gained a clearer idea of how she wanted to proceed with her poem.

Our group grew like a good marriage, with periods of blissful ease and bouts of tension. We were taken by surprise one evening during our second year when one of us erupted with, "Don't comment on my poem! I just want to read it to you!" She had grown to desire a different kind of feedback, and eventually she dropped out. As in any relationship, we needed to talk about "us." What was our vision? Were our needs met? Our dynamics became clearer, and we began to notice the unique qualities each of us brought to our sessions. Besides improving our writing, we were becoming better critics, learning to tap into our individual strengths in giving feedback. There was no self-censorship, and our ability to speak honestly created the framework for our support. Specific comments, focused on the writing itself, were not seen as personal criticism. Rather, this directness helped us to take ourselves more seriously as poets. We learned to know each other's writing and began to respond to poems as they reflected on the larger body of an individual's work.

One member moved overseas, and for the next few years we were just four women, meeting biweekly. At times during these years we again needed to discuss "us." Did our meetings take time away from our writing? Did we come to group even when we hadn't written a poem? We disagreed, grew disappointed, and even argued. It was at these times we saw ourselves as a marriage. One of us might threaten to leave, express doubt, even go home to mother for a while, but the bond we had developed through our honest and respectful interactions held. And underlying it all was the fact that each of us was still getting enormous benefit from the group. We eventually invited two women in and became six again. At public readings we called ourselves Six Voices. The ultimate achievement of our group was reflected in the name. All our time together did not make us more alike as writers. Rather, each of us had realized her own authentic voice in a way none of us could have done alone.

> We are cups, constantly and quietly being filled. The trick is knowing how to tip ourselves over and let the beautiful stuff out.
> —RAY BRADBURY

Slow Simmer vs. Microwave

Writing Group Critiques vs. Professional Workshop Deadlines

Margaret Lewis

∼

WRITING GROUP NAME: The Playwrights Collective
WRITING GROUP LOCATION: Chicago, Illinois
TYPE OF WRITERS: Playwrights and screenwriters

WRITING IS LONELY WORK. But then, if you're reading this book, you probably already know that. I, like many writers, generally try to combat the isolation and jump-start my playwriting process through classes and developmental workshops. In fact, all of my plays, except the most recent, were written under pressure of deadlines and directorial guidance. It's a great method, fast, catalytic, instantly gratifying—a sort of microwave approach to writing.

Another buffer against the isolation is belonging to a writing group. I have belonged to a terrific group called The Playwrights Collective (TPC) for about five years now. It has been a wonderful source of support, encouragement, inspiration, and the occasional badly needed butt-kicking. Until recently though, the group has not had much direct impact on my actual writing. *Creole*, my most recent play, however, was not developed through classes and workshops, and feedback from TPC played a huge part in shaping the work. This was a very different approach—longer, slower, with richer results, not unlike a stew slowly simmering in the pot.

With previous plays, perhaps because I've worked quickly to meet deadlines, it's been difficult to track the changes between versions. In *Creole*, however, the transformations are as easy to read as a fossil record, and I can trace many of the significant differences directly to TPC input. *Creole* depicts the relationship between Cora, a slave, and Lucius, the plantation owner, and TPC's support was vital to me in dealing with such a delicate subject. Responding to the group's feedback, I was able to improve everything from character development to story line to setting. Of course, much of the feedback touched upon fairly large and obvious topics, but even reactions to seemingly small things helped me think through and reshape important aspects of the play.

For example, in the first version, Cora is given a hand-carved comb by Tom, a young slave who's in love with her. Later, as Lucius seduces her, he asks about the comb, and she tells him that Tom made it for her. Members of TPC identified that as a potentially dangerous moment, something I had not earlier realized. In subsequent versions, Lucius notices the comb earlier and in a less intimate setting, and Cora evades his question about who made it, saying "It nothing special, just a comb." Lucius responds, "Someone likes you a lot, to make you something so fine," and the seeds of jealousy are planted. The comb reappears in the second act, after Cora and Lucius have become sexually involved, and fuels a fight between them.

LUCIUS

You and Tom are good friends, aren't you?

CORA

No, not really.

LUCIUS

You spend a lot of time together.

CORA

He just hang around all the time.

> (Lucius picks up Cora's hair
> comb from the nightstand.)

LUCIUS

You wear this a lot. He make it for you?

CORA

No—

LUCIUS

Don't lie to me.

The comb, originally a somewhat insignificant prop, has become a device to reveal character and forward the plot.

Feedback from the group helped me re-examine a dozen other aspects of the play, both large and small. For example, they asked me many questions about the setting, originally rather vague, and forced me to acknowledge the importance of historical accuracy and specificity. Because I was not rushing to meet a deadline, I was able to stop writing and immerse myself in further research that not only helped me nail down the setting, but that now informs each scene.

Perhaps the most profound changes in the play resulted from comments about the passivity of Cora, the main character. In the original version, Cora meekly receives attentions from both Lucius and Tom, and her emotional responses are muted. In the new version, Cora is aggressive and ambitious, actively seeking a relationship with Lucius in order to get an education and improve her status. Although she is attracted to Tom, she rejects a relationship that she knows can offer her nothing but a broken heart: "I ain't tying myself to no slave. What happens if he gets himself sold? What I supposed to do? Just stand here like a glass of curdled milk and watch him go?" Cora may now be somewhat less sympathetic, but she is a stronger, more interesting character, which in turn drives the play in a more interesting and dramatic direction.

I have noted only a few of the changes to the play, but comments from TPC have helped me rethink and reshape every character and every detail. It took me longer to write *Creole* than any of my previous plays, which was both scary and frustrating at times. And without the strong, authoritative voice of a director guiding me, I was forced to rely upon my own artistic vision, another scary situation. However, TPC was always there to support and encourage me, and the opportunity to share my work with them kept me going. (After all, what's a play without an audience?) In the end, I think *Creole* is richer, more mature, and more developed than any of my earlier work, and that is due in large measure to the slow-simmer method and the TPC test kitchen. Sometimes the slow, old-fashioned methods are best.

Favorite Resources

BOOKS

Bettelheim, Bruno. *The Uses of Enchantment: The Meaning and Importance of Fairy Tales*. New York: Vintage Books, 1989.

Egri, Lajos. *The Art of Dramatic Writing*. New York: Simon & Schuster, 1946.

Goldberg, Natalie, and Judith Guest. *Writing Down the Bones: Freeing the Writer Within*. Boston, MA: Shambhala Publications, 1986.

Sayles, John. *Thinking in Pictures*. Boston, MA: Houghton Mifflin Company, 1987.

Tobias, Ronald B. *Twenty Master Plots and How to Build Them*. Cincinnati: Writer's Digest Books, 1993.

Zipes, Jack, ed. *The Complete Fairy Tales of the Brother Grimm*. New York: Bantam Books, 1987.

———. *Tales of Wonder*. New York: Viking, 1991.

> It is the writer's business not to accuse and not to prosecute, but to champion the guilty, once they are condemned and suffer punishment.
> —ANTON CHEKHOV

Recipe for Maintaining an On-Line Writing Group

Deepa Kandaswamy

~

WRITING GROUP NAME: Writing in India

WRITING GROUP LOCATION: On-line with members in India, Australia, Ireland, the United Kingdom, Hong Kong, Canada, and the United States

TYPE OF WRITERS: Various genres

Authors are easy enough to get on with—if you are fond of children.

—MICHAEL JOSEPH

M OST WRITERS ARE like little children and if you leave them alone in a group, you have mayhem! All writers, whether they are beginners or accomplished, crave attention. But then who doesn't? The people in my on-line writing group are great but, like any group, there are those who are pessimistic, grumpy, and grouchy. We also have our optimists, cheerleaders, and those who are more sensitive. So, getting most of the people to stay active in the group, which consists mainly of freelancers from around the world, is a hard job. Writing to invisible people is another obstacle our group faces because we don't meet in the flesh.

The craft of writing is a lonely one and as someone said, "Writing is like having homework for the rest of your life." One has to keep at it and that is why so many writers join writing groups. We need to stay motivated, have people who can empathize with our plight and problems, find support (since writing is not considered a real job by most people), and develop courage. It is a nerve-racking profession that made Sydney Smith, a clergyman and writer in the early 1800s, say, "A great deal of talent is lost to the world for want of a little courage. Every day sends to their graves obscure men whose timidity prevented them from making a first effort."

Here are the six main ingredients to make a good writing group.

Networking

Personal e-mails are not allowed on the list unless they contain a critique. Most of us e-mail members off list (that is, send them a personal e-mail) if we want to get to know them better. I have found fellow writers are more comfortable talking about themselves on a one-on-one basis. The male–female composition of the group also makes many members less forthcoming when they post to the list. However, a personal e-mail works wonders. Many members even send you their family portrayals/narratives.

Exercises

We have weekly exercises set up by the members of the list. This serves three purposes. First, it keeps the members on their toes and their creative juices flowing. Second, the member who sets the exercise feels he/she is able to control the list even if it is only for a short time. This fosters a sense of responsibility and belonging. Third, all writers like to display their work to get instant gratification when some other member on the list likes it or critiques it in a positive manner.

Sharing/Bragging Week

Every month, the last week is set aside for sharing market information; stories of our publishing success; links to writers' articles if available; agent information; information about current projects; calls for help; contact details and other research information; and horror stories about particular publications. We cheer each other on and give each other virtual pats on the back.

Discussion

If something is bothering a member of the group, such as dealing with a rejection slip or powerlessness to deal with personal loss of a loved one, then members are free to post it for discussion. This instills a sense of community among members. I have found discussions get lively and extremely informative if they are on the subject of writing itself, especially writer's woes. (Why are editors insensitive? Are we really writing for money or passion, as many in the group don't believe in writing for free? Is it worthwhile to participate in writing contests which charge entry/reading fees? And much more.)

Questions

Most beginners are encouraged to ask questions. They think their questions won't be considered intelligent enough, because they are not very familiar with such terms as *kill fee* or the difference between a sidebar and a side box, and so on. I have found all writers have questions on copyright issues, and because the list includes writers from around the world we compare notes. And there is always the question of means/modes of payment.

Concern

It's always amazing to me that writers, who can make something mundane like fishing sound extremely romantic, get bogged down when it comes to our own lives. But an occasional "Are you OK?" e-mail on the list makes us extremely happy. Support and kindness to fellow scribes is essential. I've found this helps all writers, especially the older writers who are the most appreciative.

~

Maintaining a group is very much like managing friendships. To stop writers from unsubscribing to the group they need individual attention; pats on the back; prompt responses; a little empathy; and honest, intelligent, and gentle critiques.

The final but secret ingredient is trust. In my experience, face-to-face writing group meetings aren't important as long as writers feel they can trust the other group members.

Mix all these ingredients together and you will not only have a writing group, but you'll also have fun!

Favorite Resources

WEB SITES

http://freereads.topcities.com

www.absolutewrite.com

www.burryman.com

www.freelancing4money.com

www.inscriptionsmagazine.com

www.smartgroups.com/vault/michaellarocca

www.writebytes.co.uk

www.writersdigest.com

www.writersweekly.com

www.writethinking.net

www.writing-world.com

www.writingfordollars.com

FAVORITE WRITING EXERCISES

■ SENTENCE STORY. Write an entire story in a single sentence.

■ STEREOTYPE. In 500 words or less, write a story where a character is presented in a stereotypical way. As the story unfolds have the stereotype turn out to be erroneous by revealing either the location or the character's true nature.

■ AS YOU WISH. Submit any article that you are currently struggling with to the group for their comments and suggestions.

■ HEADLINES. Pick up a news headline from print, television, or the Internet and write your own nonfiction piece in 500 words or less.

■ VENT. Write a 250-word article venting your depression, anger, or outrage on an issue or person you feel strongly about. If you feel like whining, do it with flare and use good imagery.

> **Those who write clearly have readers, those who write obscurely have commentators.**
> —ALBERT CAMUS

Keep Your Mouth Shut

The Key to Getting Helpful Critiques

JOHN WEAGLY

~

WRITING GROUP NAME: Untitled

WRITING GROUP LOCATION: Chicago, Illinois

TYPE OF WRITERS: Playwrights, screenwriters, novelists, and short story writers

YOU'VE FINISHED YOUR PLAY. Congratulations! You've been slaving away over a hot keyboard for months and now it's finally done. You have visions of sold-out houses, rave reviews, and a Tony Award dancing through your head.

So what's your next step? Obviously, you need to get the darn thing produced, but is it ready to be produced? How can you find out if your vision is stageworthy?

One of the easiest things you can do is join a writing group. This can be a group made up of fellow playwrights or, even better, writers from all walks of life. While it's a good idea to have a couple of other playwrights in the group, it's also beneficial to have novelists, journalists, and other kinds of writers involved. This way, you can see how your play works for people who don't know that much about theater. These are the people who aren't going to worry about things like stage directions, the number of actors your script needs, and what can or can't be accomplished on a struggling theater's small budget. These are the people who are going to talk about plot points and character development and whether or not your play makes sense.

Now, don't get me wrong, other playwrights are going to comment on all of these aspects of your script, but the non-playwrights are going to give you different points of view.

OK, you've joined a writing group. Now what do you do? Now, you keep your mouth shut.

One of the most common problems in writing groups is too much talk from the playwright who's having his/her script critiqued. As a piece is being discussed, there's a strong temptation to interrupt and refute every comment made with an explanation. When someone says, "It doesn't make sense to have Gloria leave so early," the playwright answers with, "I did that because she was disgusted with everyone in the room." This kind of reaction only slows down the progress of the group with needless discussion and, more often than not, an argument. More importantly, it doesn't matter!

Of course you the playwright know why Gloria left, but if it doesn't make sense in the script, then it doesn't make sense. What's written on the page is the only thing that matters; the writer shouldn't have to explain the logic behind his or her choices. If you were going for something specific, but the other people in the group didn't get it, you need to consider doing it another way. When you send your play off to a theater, you're not going to be sitting next to the artistic director when he or she reads it. You're not going to be able to explain what's going on in the script. The only thing that affects the story is what is written on the page.

When your fellow writers are done discussing your work, ask questions. You can ask, "Why didn't it make sense to have Gloria leave so early?" or "How can I make it make sense for Gloria to leave so early?" Or, you can ask nothing at all. Remember, you don't have to use all, or even any of the suggestions made by your writing group cohorts. You may not agree with something someone says, but just say "thank you" and move on. It's your play; every decision will ultimately be yours.

Explaining what's happening in your play is like telling the people that were kind enough to comment on your work that they are wrong to have their opinions. And, you may not think so at the time, but in a couple of days you might realize that they were on to something.

So how should you behave at your writing group meetings? Don't explain. Be thankful. And keep your mouth shut.

Favorite Resources

BOOKS

Vogler, Christopher. *The Writer's Journey: Mythic Structure for Storytellers and Screenwriters*. Studio City, CA: Michael Wiese Productions, 1998. Information: (818) 379-8799 or www.mwp.com.
It's about the hero's journey—what the different milestones and obstacles are. It helps me a lot with structure.

WEB SITES

www.horror.org
The Official Horror Writer's Association Newsletter goes out monthly to members of the Horror Writer's Association. This is

also good for keeping current on short story markets. It features great articles for writers. Information: newsletter@horror.org.

www.johnweagly.com

www.performink.com
*Perform*Ink is Chicago's theater and film industry biweekly newpaper.

www.Ralan.com
Ralan's Webstravaganza. Great for keeping current on markets for short stories.

Twilight Tales Reading Series
Tina@TwilightTales.com
www.TwilightTales.com
Twilight Tales is a weekly reading series held Monday nights at the Red Lion Pub in Chicago. The first Monday of the month is open-mike night. People read work in every genre—stories, essays, plays, poetry. There's no official discussion or feedback session, but it's a great place to go and be around like-minded creative people.

WORKSHOP

ALGIS BUDRYS WORKSHOP

Algis is a Chicago-based, fairly well-known writer and editor in the science fiction field. I've seen him give his presentation on how to put together a plot on a couple of different occasions and it's always a great reminder of the basics.

Climbing Out of the Snake Pit

A Writing Group Clears a Path to Healing

SUSAN REULING FURNESS, WRITING AND POETRY THERAPIST

~

WRITING GROUP NAME: The Write Path

WRITING GROUP LOCATION: Boise, Idaho

TYPE OF WRITERS: Fiction, nonfiction, poets, newspaper columnists, inspirational, memoirists, essayists, personal reflection

> **"Writing . . . has been a sturdy ladder out of a deep pit."**
> —ALICE WALKER

A GROUP OF NERVOUS WRITERS come clutching journals, gnawing on pens. Assembling in my office, they will spend the early weeks developing trust for each other and learning to silence their internal editors. I assume my work with this group is straightforward. I will tease their creative juices. I will cheer their self-confidence. I will nourish their voices on the page. I am prepared to do this work.

Or am I?

Rob* is one of the eight. I know his problems are thorny. He had an affair. I also know that when the fur flew at home, Rob recommitted to his marriage. Still he courts the other woman in his mind. As a result, his self-respect is in the toilet. I recommended the writing group, but I did not foresee the writing collision between Rob and another writer, Josephine.

During the third session, Rob pens a poem divulging the mental adultery he commits daily. The eyes of the other writers show compassion. Josephine reads next. I do not anticipate her story about another infidel, her husband, who continues to cheat. As Jo's story unfolds, I feel apprehension rivet the room. The Golden Gate Bridge stands with less tension than holds this group together. "Dear God," I muttered, "What do I do now?"

~

Sherry's husband did not recommit after his affair. She writes with the Tuesday morning group. In the second week of the ten-week session, she details her tears of loneliness and despair. But in the fourth session, while sitting cross-legged on her chair, Sherry reads, "My family is on the lam." I think the phrase is poetic. "My five children left with my husband," she concludes. The temperature in the room drops forty degrees.

"Oh my God!" I whisper, "What now? This is no metaphor!"

*All names and situations of the clients mentioned in this chapter have been changed to protect their privacy.

~

This is what I do for a living. I walk a precarious scaffold to help others build a stairway to self-confidence. It's a scary business. Sometimes I stop breathing as the drama unfolds.

I stumbled onto this career path by dumb luck. Just as Alice Walker found "a sturdy ladder out of a deep pit," I learned firsthand how writing leads the way to a better life, a better me.

In September 1998, I was a nonwriter in search of something. God knows what. But both God and I knew I was bored as a therapist. This was my second or third career, depending on how you counted, and my creativity was languishing. Though many consider counseling an art form, I found myself increasingly restless. A friend suggested I might like to write. "Ha!" my reticent skeptic replied. "Yeah!" my inner artiste shouted. So it was, that I soon sat in a "Write from the Heart" workshop in New Mexico.

Joan Logghe, an accomplished poet, sat draped in a mauve shawl. She looked ethereal as we began. "Write freely, quickly, without concern for grammar, structure, or form," she said. And so I did. After the first exercise, we read aloud. The first two readers, Camille and Laurie, delivered print-ready masterpieces. I soon realized that the group consisted of five professional writers, a retired Presbyterian minister, and me. My confidence retreated and a familiar, pig-headed self-doubt rushed to the forefront. *What was I thinking? I'm just a therapist. Get me out of here!*

But somehow I stayed. On the second day, my writing felt bolder. As a storm rattled outside, the group leader suggested that we use a repetitive form to write about anger. OK, I can do this, I thought. Truthful, congruent words flowed from my pen like water over Niagara Falls.

The story I wrote portrayed my life with the evil trolls—my critical family and friends. I laced the story with some well-chosen expletives to demonstrate the depth of my anger. As I finished reading, the graying vicar pushed his glasses atop his forehead. Apparently he did not remember the "no criticism" rule. He spoke. "It seems a shame for a lovely woman to use such vile language."

Arrgh!—a dagger to my heart—acid on my tiny crumb of confidence. I wanted to bolt again.

Yet somewhere from the depth of my unconscious, poetry nudged me. I do not remember the next assignment. Instead, my racing mind fixated on the anger I felt about this new censure. The pen sliced the paper as a rhyming tirade exploded in my head. At the next pause for reading, I looked straight into the eyes of the cleric and read "The Censor." My voice was strong.

Deliverance! The clumsy poem, and the simple act of reading it, defeated an entire legion of critics. I spoke, not just to this stranger, but to all the fault-finding quibblers in my life. My unbridled pen had cut beneath the layers of social norms and told the angry, unedited truth. That truth led me from a snake pit of intimidation. I was free. I had signed on for a writing group, but I knew *this* was therapy.

I also knew, in that moment, I could help men and women find confidence through writing. I would create an oasis for thirsting people back home.

~

As a group leader, I watch pens scratch words of disillusionment, secrecy, and shame. Writing helps soothe these dark, dark feelings. Paper and pen carry the writer toward hope and creativity. But sometimes a writer like Sherry or Josephine falls flat onto parched desert sand. How do I manage the unforeseen hazards? What if a whole group tumbles into a bottomless pit?

~

The writers tiptoe into my office on September 12, 2001. They begin writing from a prompt on the board. After twenty minutes, I interrupt the silence, "Find a place to stop. It is time to share what you have written."

Patty, one of the first to arrive, volunteers to read. She begins, "Kevin and Sean were on top. The fire is still burning. The boys are still missing." Reality sets in slowly. Patty's nephews were on the 104th floor of yesterday's catastrophe in New York City.

"Oh dear God!" I mutter under my breath. "*Can* I proceed?"

I had known that facilitating groups would not be easy today. I wrestled with my plans last evening, trashing the suddenly trite "Conformity or Creativity?" theme. I fumbled through resources until I landed on a Gandhi quote for the whiteboard. *Terrorism and deception are weapons, not of the strong but of the weak.* The quote would work. Beyond that, I could only hope people would write what they needed to write.

They did. Patty did. Everyone did. Their heartfelt words spoke to the reality of the day. The journals candidly chronicled fear, grief, bewilderment, anger, and total disbelief. The writing recycled memories from other disasters—Oklahoma City, Beirut, Hanoi. Group members revisited grisly accident scenes, catastrophes, and deaths.

~

To tell the truth, being a writing and poetry therapist terrorizes me. Debris lies under the skin of every writer. An innocent writing prompt can detonate a nuclear bomb for an individual or an entire group.

Still I have learned to trust that words will show the way out of any pit. Writing in a journal will relieve the pain and confusion for anyone who will pick up a pen or pencil. I trust writing to the bottom of my toes. Even when I am baffled as a leader, another round of writing will show the writers to emotional safety and sanity again.

And so it was that on September 12, 2001, I trusted a favorite healing exercise. I call this one "Change the Channel." It works every time. On September 12, we wrote from the dark side for nearly ninety minutes. The group *needed* to address the horror and despair. But I also knew I could not leave them on the smoke and ashes channel. Near the end of the session, I took the leap of faith to lighten the airwaves.

"Feelings are like stray cats," I began. "They will sleep on your doorstep, but if you don't feed them, they will move on. I know you need to acknowledge these heavy feelings," I continued, "but now that we've spent some time with despair, I want you to write the word *hope* at the top of your page. Then put your pen on the paper and see what happens."

Pens flew across the journal pages. I held my breath. I wondered if the group believed this assignment was insensitive. But when we read, the reception was clearer and brighter. Patty wrote an ode to heroes. Tim wrote a letter to compassion. Someone painted a relief, by describing a day on the mountain. The despair lifted, at least for the moment. Hope lived again.

One poignant word, a simple prompt, helped these writers climb out of the snake pit of despair. Hope lived for Patty and the others, just as courage was uncovered for Rob, Josephine, and Sherry with a "Change the Channel" assignment. Indeed, there was no need to panic. There never is. Writing will show the way, if only we trust paper and pen.

> I read and walked for miles at night along the beach, writing bad blank verse and searching endlessly for someone wonderful who would step out of the darkness and change my life. It never crossed my mind that person could be me.
> —ANNA QUINDLEN

Favorite Resources

BOOKS

Adams, Kathleen, M.A., L.P.C. *The Way of the Journal*. Lutherville, MD: The Sidran Press, 1998.

Bender, Sheila. *Keeping a Journal You Love*. Cincinnati, OH: Walking Stick Press, 2001.

Cameron, Julia. *The Artist's Way: Spiritual Path to Higher Creativity*. New York: C.P. Putnam and Sons, 1992.

———. *The Right to Write: An Invitation and Initiation into the Writing Life*. New York: Tarcher/Putman, 1998.

DeSalvo, Lousie. *Writing as a Way of Healing: How Telling Our Stories Transforms Our Lives*. San Francisco: Harper Books, 1999.

Dreamer, Oriah Mountain. *The Invitation*. San Francisco: HarperCollins, 1999.

Fox, John. *Finding What You Didn't Lose: Expressing Your Truth and Creativity Through Poem-Making*. New York: Tarcher/Putnam, 1995.

Goldberg, Natalie. *Wild Mind: Living the Writer's Life*. New York: Bantam Books, 1990.

————, and Judith Guest. *Writing Down the Bones: Freeing the Writer Within*. Boston, MA: Shambhala Publications, 1986.

Hynes, Arleen McCarthy, and Mary Hynes-Berry. *Biblio/Poetry Therapy—The Interactive Process: A Handbook*. St. Cloud, MN: North Star Press of St. Cloud, Inc., 1994.

Klauser, Henrietta Anne. *Write It Down, Make It Happen*. New York: Fireside Books, Simon & Schuster, 2000.

Koch, Kenneth. *I Never Told Anybody: Teaching Writing in a Nursing Home*. New York: Random House, 1977.

Lamott, Anne. *Bird by Bird: Some Instructions on Writing and Life*. New York: Anchor Books, 1995.

Metcalf, Linda Trichter, and Tobin Simon. *Writing the Mind Alive: The Proprioceptive Method for Finding Your Authentic Voice*. New York: Ballantine Books, 2002.

Pennebaker, James. Ph.D. *Opening Up: The Healing Power of Expressing Emotions*. New York: The Guilford Press, 1990.

Remen, Rachel Naomi, M.D. *Kitchen Table Wisdom: Stories That Heal*. New York: Berkley Publishing Group, 1996.

Roorbach, Bill. *Writing Life Stories*. Cincinnati, OH: Story Press, 1998.

Sagan, Marim. *Unbroken Line: Writing in the Lineage of Poetry*. Santa Fe, NM: Sherman Asher Publishing, 1999.

Schiwy, Marlene A. *A Voice of Her Own: Women and the Journal Writing Journey*. New York: Fireside Books, Simon & Schuster, 1996.

Wooldridge, Susan G. *Poemcrazy: Freeing Your Life with Words*. New York: Three Rivers Press, 1996.

Yalom, Irvin D. *The Theory and Practice of Group Psychotherapy*. Third edition. New York: Basic Books, 1985.

PART III

WHY WRITING GROUPS FLOURISH OR FIZZLE

■

It's exactly when people try to figure out what pigeonhole they belong in that they kill their work. I borrow from everything that turns me on. If that makes me 'post-modernist,' so be it.

—ERIC BOGOSIAN, playwright, performance artist, and much more

Writing groups flourish by continuing to find new ways to be valuable to members. Cohesion grows out of shared experiences. Going to another group member's book signing or play reading, attending conferences together, or planning a writing retreat can help your writing group endure. Groups that welcome change will flourish. Some groups, however, fizzle due to their own good intentions, while others suffer from members outgrowing the organizing principles of the group. Some grow stagnant because they fail to add new members. Here are essays that invite you to learn from the triumphs and tragedies of other writing groups.

A Good Group Is Hard to Find

ELLEN BIRKETT MORRIS

~

WRITING GROUP NAME: Untitled

WRITING GROUP LOCATION: Louisville, Kentucky

TYPE OF WRITERS: Children's authors, poets, and novelists

LIKE MOST WRITERS, I've heard my share of horror stories about writing groups.

I was afraid I'd end up in a group of writers whose work I didn't respect, who followed the lead of a dictatorial facilitator, who spent hours chatting about personal matters, or who lacked the insight into the craft to help my work along.

I was like a divorcee at a crowded singles bar when I first started looking for a writing group. I was convinced I'd never find Mr. Right.

I've come to believe a good writing group is like a good spouse and should meet several criteria.

1. **Are these people you want to spend time with?** Do you find the members of the group to be friendly and interesting? Are they easy to talk to? If you got locked in an elevator with them after a meeting could you stand to wait for the emergency rescue squad? Could you handle an

eight-hour car trip with these folks? That was my bottom line in choosing a spouse.

2. **Are they roughly as smart as you are?** Or are they NASCAR to your *New Yorker*? Like a good husband, a good writing group should not be afraid to expand their worldview. You want a group that will understand your allusions and get the larger cultural framework in which your work is set.

3. **Do they have a decent sense of humor?** The first time my husband helped me laugh at myself I knew he had a lifetime lock on my love. Let's face it, our writing (and our quality of life) suffers when we take ourselves too seriously and can't laugh at our foibles. Every group has a Comma Queen and an Earl of Adjectives. Frank discussion and a few laughs can help us clean up our prose and become better writers.

4. **Are they good communicators?** Do they know how to offer constructive feedback in a diplomatic way? I know my husband will be straight with me when I get a really bad haircut. I'm grateful for the chance to see another hairdresser and make things right. No matter how much you like each other, you need a group committed to giving and receiving honest feedback on the work. If all you want is praise you could just send the piece to your mother and be through with it.

5. **Do they love writing with a true heart and without reservation?** My husband loves me just the way I am, not some idealized version of me. You want a group of people committed to writing, not fascinated with the idea of

being a writer. You want to be surrounded by people who have spent hours reading, soaking in the language, and looking for what works.

I kept looking for the perfect group and kept my standards high. I'm happy to say I've found a writing group that fits the bill.

Before you ask, the answer is no. You can't have their phone numbers.

> **This is not a novel to be tossed aside lightly. It should be thrown with great force.**
> —DOROTHY PARKER

Ten Reasons Why Writing Groups Flounder, Fizzle, or Fail

KATHY BRICCETTI

~

WRITING GROUP NAME: Untitled

WRITING GROUP LOCATION: Berkeley, California

TYPE OF WRITERS: Essayists, memoirists, fiction and nonfiction writers

HAS YOUR WRITING GROUP morphed into a coffee hour or book club? Did it fizzle out completely and you're still not sure why? Or perhaps your current group is losing momentum. For any stage of a writing group's life, avoid these ten situations to stay on track and remain productive.

- **Members use the group for the wrong reason.** For newcomers and old-timers both, it's important to acknowledge what a writing group is *not*. A writing group is not a social hour, literary discussion group, or book club. If a group slips into one of these functions, members may in fact be avoiding writing or the risk of sharing their writing with others. It may be that the group lacks a structure, a format for meetings, which keeps members critiquing, improving, and producing work. A writing group is not group therapy. Yes, a writing group can provide considerable support and a feeling of camaraderie as members forge new ground in their creative work. Like group therapy, a writing group is a place where members often bare their souls, and even make life changes, but the goal is to improve writing. Finally, a writing group is not a place to show off, compete, or impress. Rather it's a place to remain humble and open to constructive criticism. It's a place to work and grow.

- **Critiques are too harsh.** Groups without enough safety rules, containment, or a reliable structure can slip into ruthless, abrasive criticism. Faced with insensitive or callous feedback, members are likely to feel hurt or insulted and race out the door. Successful groups feel supportive and nurturing, not threatening.

- **Critiques are too positive.** On the other hand, groups can suffer from the Pollyanna syndrome, with members handing out sweeping statements of praise and love that don't move the writer toward improving through revision. Critiques need to be honest. If members feel they are wasting their time, they're sure to drop out. Critiques need to balance praise and constructive criticism, both gentle and specific.

- **Members drop out before the group gels.** When people join any type of group, they tend to look for ways they are different and won't fit in. In a writing group a new member may fear her writing doesn't measure up to the rest of the group, or on the opposite end of the spectrum, may disdain less experienced writers. The early stages of any group are the most challenging. Recognizing that groups take time to settle down, get comfortable, and trust each other, members may want to agree to a trial period, to stick it out for three or six months and evaluate the group's effectiveness and potential then.

- **There are varying levels of commitment to writing.** Some groups may find themselves with members who are less committed to writing than others. Some groups ban those who are not writing. Others allow them to remain if they continue to provide critique. Others schedule critiques in order to provide nudges and discipline. Writers need writing groups more at different times in their careers. Members need to recognize when they need the support and when they should leave for a time.

- **Attendance is sporadic.** Members should commit to attending every meeting except in the case of illness, emergencies, and vacations. This is particularly important at the beginning of a group's life when continuity, connection between members, and regular feedback on work can get the group off to a good start and keep it productive.

- **Sessions focus on the content, not the writing.** Writing groups need to focus on the strengths and weaknesses of the writing and not get waylaid by the content of the piece or, in the case of memoir, the writer's life. Don't second-guess the writer's intention; instead concentrate on what the writing conveyed to you. Maintain a friendly but businesslike atmosphere by keeping comments impersonal.

Don't share what the piece under scrutiny reminds you of in literature, the movies, or your own life.

- **There is poor personal chemistry between members.** If one or two people dominate, compete, or show off, this needs to be addressed either in a written or verbal evaluation of the group's strengths and weaknesses or in a clarification of meeting structure and expectations. Direct dialogue and review of rules and goals may be necessary. Someone might tactfully approach a troublesome member and request a change, or as a last resort, the group may need to disband and reform minus a member or two.

- **Members don't appreciate the different styles and abilities of the group.** Writers' varying abilities and experience should not be excessively disparate (e.g., beginning writers and book authors), but some variety is healthy and mutually beneficial. Whatever the makeup of the group, members need to respect the goals of other writers' work. Almost every serious writer, at any stage of his or her career, has something to contribute. And finally, members—novices or pros—can almost always learn from critiques of others' pieces.

- **There is jealousy and competitiveness.** A group that doesn't feel safe enough for members to support each other toward success—whether it's publishing, winning a contest, or reaching a personal goal—will ultimately fail. Acknowledge that envy is normal, but let it spur you toward improvement. Don't let your group fall into back-biting or ruthless competition. Delight in the pleasure of each other's achievements and cheer each other on by sharing marketing leads, rejections, and successes. After all, the group can take some credit too when writers experience success.

By recognizing and avoiding these writing group pitfalls you can enliven your current group, resuscitate a terminal one, or start fresh with a greater chance of group longevity and productivity. Good luck!

Favorite Resources

BOOKS

Barrington, Judith. *Writing the Memoir*. Portland, OR: Eighth Mountain Press, 1997.

Elbow, Peter. *Writing Without Teachers*. New York: Oxford University Press, 1973.

Haines, Dawn Denham; Susan Newcomer; and Jacqueline Raphael. *Writing Together: How to Transform Your Writing in Writing Group*. New York: Perigee Books, 1997.

Lamott, Anne. *Bird by Bird: Some Instructions on Writing and Life*. New York: Anchor Books, 1995.

LeGuin, Ursula. *Steering the Craft*. Portland, OR: The Eighth Mountain Press, 1998.

Schneider, Pat. *The Writer as an Artist*. New York: Lowell House, 1993.

ON-LINE WRITING GROUP, CLASSES, CRITIQUE SERVICES

www.craigslist.org
Craig's List
Activity partners and writing groups are arranged by major cities.

www.manistee.com/~lkraus/workshop
The Internet Writing Workshop
This on-line writing group's organized by genre: fiction, nonfiction, novels, poetry, script, young adult, love story, prose, practice, and teen write. Submit pieces for critique and critique others' work from home. Members often receive feedback within days. You can also join a writing discussion group. No charge.

www.pw.org
Poets & Writers on-line offers classes. Information: (212) 226-3586.

www.writersdigest.com
Writer's Digest offers an on-line criticism service. There is a fee. Information: (513) 531-2690.

> **Write down all the stuff you swore you'd never tell another soul.**
> —ANNE LAMOTT

The Retreat

K AREN P ROPP

~

WRITING GROUP NAME: Jill
WRITING GROUP LOCATION: Cambridge, Massachusetts
TYPE OF WRITERS: Fiction writers and essayists

T EN YEARS AGO, when my writing group met in a newly rented apartment, a place as dark as it was cheap, the idea grabbed hold of us to plan a writing retreat. Mary first suggested the idea, or was it Pagan, whose then-boyfriend's father had a rambling summer house in Maine? "Everyone will begin a novel," I proposed. "And finish it in a weekend," Pagan added. The assignment was so preposterous we could only laugh. "Just page counts," said Lauren. "No self-censoring. Straight from the id."

It turned out to be just the right amount of competition. There was this finish line—writing a novel in a weekend—that no one could reach, but at the same time we would vie with one another in friendly sport to get as far along as was humanly possible.

The stars must've been lined up that August: the boyfriend's father who had a home in Maine said yes, everyone's schedule was accommodating, and on that memorable weekend, the sky was clear and sunny. During the two-hour drive from Boston to Maine, talk was plentiful. Money and mothers and dating. Therapists and rejection slips. Gynecology and interior decorating, two subjects that are not as disparate as you might think. "I once knew a man," I mumbled somewhere around Pembroke. "Maybe I could write about him, about that. . . ."

When I woke in the morning, I could hear the lapping sea. Salty air breezed through the windows. I padded down to the kitchen and made myself a cup of coffee and reveled in the quiet—so full of possibility, so many pages waiting to be written! It helped that the house was large and rambling and filled with comfortable cushions, faded Indian bedspreads. But here's the crux of why our writing retreat worked so well: we worked in proximity to one another. Writing is a lonely occupation, and sometimes that loneliness can squelch one's fluency as much as any other force. But for that weekend, we'd found just the right amount of solitude and support. I sat at a narrow desk in an upstairs bedroom and wrote longhand in a bound notebook. Lauren sat up in bed, tapping furiously at her laptop. Pagan sat staring at her computer in a downstairs room behind French doors, and Mary sat on a large boulder at the beach, the wind blowing her skirts, writing in an unlined artists' pad. Hearing the tap tap tap of one friend's fingers on her keyboard, seeing another's concentrated stare, just knowing the others were being productive propelled me to do the same.

After all, there was the page count contest. We'd agreed to weigh in that evening, like pigs at the county fair. The page count contest was meant to lower standards and generate material. We were all experts at explicating the word; all writing program workshop graduates with years of fine-tuning our critical capacities, and this weekend was meant to be a departure from that self-conscious looking over one's shoulder stuff. This weekend was meant to be a liberation of our creative powers, an unlocking of stream-of-consciousness, a discovery draft written at breakneck speed.

Late afternoon, as the light began to ebb, we weighed in with our page counts. Seventeen pages. Nineteen pages. Twenty-seven. Thirty-two. More than any of us had written before in a single, solitary day.

The boyfriend and his friends cooked for us: lobster and corn on the cob and spaghetti and salad and beer and wine. We writers did the dishes. Then we sprawled on couches and rugs to listen to what each person had written that day.

Was it the wine or the sea or the sheer euphoria of having spewed out so many words at one sitting? Perhaps it was the camaraderie and the sense that we were all in this together. Or the honing in on one's id rather than ego. Maybe it was the pact that we'd made: to write as much as we could and then read it aloud, no judgments passed.

~

Here I should digress to say that as a rule we are not a group that works with photocopied manuscripts. Instead, we always read aloud. We read aloud to encourage feedback that is spontaneous and responsive; because it strengthens the voice and sharpens the ear and because we believe that writing, ultimately, is a social contract. We read aloud because we'd rather listen to the gut and flow of the piece than micromanage the word. And because we are too impatient and cheap to wait in line to copy, staple, and distribute, and too vulnerable to cope with that ominous rustling of paper after a piece is read, that sharply critical sound made worse by polite coughs and a silence that goes on a millisecond too long.

~

That evening, after the lobster and sun, after the silence and salt spray, the readings were accompanied by more than one laughing apology. It's difficult to resort to artifice when you are writing that fast and at the same time it's easier to be honest.

~

That evening, a certain standard was set within the group, a standard that has held us in good stead all these many weeks and months and years since the retreat. You can lower your standards and go for broke. You are capable of doing more than you think. If you are willing to fail you can also fly.

Two of us went home after that weekend and lickety-split finished the novels we'd begun. We continue to write fast and read aloud, and by these methods we have cumulatively published two novels, six memoirs, four nonfiction books, one short story collection, fifty magazine articles, and five pieces in Best American Essays. We have won an Orange Prize nomination, an NEA grant, two National Magazine Award nominations, and two grants from the Massachusetts Cultural Council.

We'd like to go on another retreat, but the house in Maine is no longer available.

Staying Together

A Bond of Focus and Respect

Marnie Brooks

~

WRITING GROUP NAME: Triangle Circle
WRITING GROUP LOCATION: Raleigh, North Carolina
TYPE OF WRITERS: Children's writers of poetry, short stories, nonfiction, young adult, middle grade, picture books, and science fiction/fantasy

WE'VE ALL HEARD horror stories of battered egos, scarred muses, and feuds instigated by writing groups. Yet others have been together for years with members landing multibook contracts and establishing lifelong friendships.

What's the secret to a successful group? Some might say Karma, magic, or serendipity, and others avow hard work. Maybe it's all of these elements combined with a complementary blend of personalities that define a group's dynamics and longevity. I believe it depends on individuals' commitment to their craft, themselves, and their fellow members. Respect is also a key factor—regard for your own work as well as that of others.

Although I write for adults and children, I belong to a children's writing group. This shared focus brought us together—

strangers attracted by a newspaper ad—and has kept us cohesive and successful for a decade. We evolved from a one-facilitator, one-meeting-place group of five writers to a flexible team that takes turns hosting meetings and facilitating so that everyone knows how to run a group and encourage productivity. It's been a trial-and-error process and we continue to refine it to accommodate new members and changing goals.

We call ourselves the Triangle Circle. We meet once a month and have ten members. Attendance varies depending on life, work, or family obligations, but six or seven come on a regular basis. Members are male and female with ages ranging from forty-five to eighty. Three members are illustrator/writers, which offers a unique perspective for others who write only. We create a variety of books within our genre including picture books, middle-grade and young adult novels, nonfiction, poetry, science fiction/fantasy, and short stories.

While we have day jobs or are retired from them, we have gained success throughout the years with achievements ranging from publishing in magazines and newspapers to multibook contracts, national awards, and favorable reviews in *Publisher's Weekly*. Membership in our group does not depend on whether someone is published; it is contingent on the person's commitment to the genre, regular attendance, and a professional attitude.

I've been asked, "How have you stayed together so long?" Truthfully, I feel blessed. However, our varied scope of interests keeps us stimulated and allows us to bring different views to a critique through our areas of "expertise." Our critiquing methods also include e-mail and telephone when members travel or can't make meetings due to schedule conflicts. In this way we're able to keep lines of communication and encouragement open among all members. We have become friends sharing in births, deaths, successes, and failures. We have a yearly holiday gathering for social time and catching up with members on the move.

The muse is not an easy master and writing for children is not child's play. There are constraints to plot complexities, subject matter, age-appropriate dialogue, and length. Most important, children's writers must learn *not* to write *down* to kids. Children are perceptive, discerning readers (and listeners) and can detect preaching no matter how well authors disguise it. But kids are also ardent fans who can offer enthusiastic adoration as well as brutal honesty.

Respect for children's writers from adult genre writers and some of the naïve general public is not often forthcoming, which is another reason why we need serious writing support. There's nothing more teeth-grinding than the comment, "So you write for children—how sweet."

While genre may be the glue that holds some groups together, there has to be more to weather the inevitable conflicts that come from a union of creative individuals with myriad personalities, desires, goals, and interests. I'm not a psychologist or veteran of numerous groups, but I can share what works for us and may for others—no matter what genre a writer pursues.

Below are Triangle Circle's shared goals, motivations, and rules, which we have developed to keep ourselves joyful, inspired, and productive.

Shared Goals

- Strive to become better writers and help others do the same.

- Share each other's successes with grace and enthusiasm.

- Listen to critiques with mouths shut and ears open.

- Meet monthly at the same time, but be flexible to accommodate changing schedules.

- Attend meetings whether you have something for critique or not; make it part of your writing commitment.

- Respect your craft, yourself, and other members and their efforts.

- Network in the field and share marketing information such as editorial needs/experiences, agent insights, and industry news.

- Stay current on trends and publishers' lists.

- Keep tuned for information that might help another's work or goal.

- Be open to new members, but keep the group to no more than ten.

- Read, read, and read some more.

- Love what you do and you will succeed!

Motivation

- When a member becomes stalled on a project, others help by encouraging the writer to consider plot snags, character motivation, or whatever might get the person over the hump.

- Take a professional attitude toward your writing and the work of others.

- Strive to bring something to read, discuss, or brainstorm at each meeting.

- Offer encouragement (or commiseration) on rejections, but make sure the rejected writer leaves with a positive attitude or something to work on for revision.

- Come to each group ready to work, listen, share, and learn.

- Don't be afraid to push the envelope with your writing and help others do the same.

- Respect the joy of writing and encourage your muse in creative ways.

- Look for conference, workshop, and promotional opportunities.

- Support other members at book signings, speaking engagements, and so on, whenever possible.

- Bring champagne and chocolate to celebrate successes!

Rules

- Leave egos at the door.

- Be prompt or let others know you'll be late so that the meeting may begin to make sure all who wish critiques can be heard.

- Critique the piece, not the person.

- Use what you can from a critique and lose what doesn't work for you.

- Point out positive areas as well as those that might need work.

- Allow another critic to finish before you speak.

- Critiquees should not defend their work, but are welcome to ask questions about comments.

- Be aware of time constraints so that everyone who wishes feedback has a chance.

- The member who is hosting the meeting is the facilitator for the session.

- The facilitator's role is to serve as the timekeeper, keep discussions on track, and mediate if there are conflicts.

- Give hugs when needed!

Favorite Resources

BOOKS

King, Stephen. *On Writing: A Memoir of the Craft*. New York: Scribner, 2000.

Lamott, Anne. *Bird by Bird: Some Instructions on Writing and Life*. New York: Anchor Books, 1995.

MAGAZINES

Children's Writer. Children's Institute of Literature, 93 Long Ridge Road, West Redding, CT 06896-1124.

Children's Writer Guide to the Marketplace (annual). Children's Institute of Literature, 93 Long Ridge Road, West Redding, CT 06896-1124.

SCBWI National Bulletin. 8271 Beverly Boulevard, Los Angeles, CA 90048.

Writer's Digest. 4700 East Galbraith Road, Cincinnati, OH 45236.

> Whenever you write, whatever you write, never make the mistake of assuming the audience is any less intelligent than you are.
> —ROD SERLING

Working Together in a Novel Way

Joan Marie Verba

~

WRITING GROUP NAME: Aaardvark Writing Group

WRITING GROUP LOCATION: Minnetonka, Minnesota

TYPE OF WRITERS: Science fiction, fantasy, and mystery writers

THE AAARDVARK WRITING GROUP (the extra *a* is for alphabetic advantage), founded more than twenty years ago, helps its members to grow and succeed as authors. We have reached our goals and maintained our progress through style, support, common interests, diverse experiences, teamwork, and outreach.

A few things make our group distinctive. First, we're all imaginative fiction writers. Second, each author reads her work aloud at meetings (among other benefits, this definitively reveals whether the dialogue sounds genuine). Third, while many writing groups require the author to be silent during critique, we don't. Fourth, because our group is so diverse—members have degrees in English, mathematics, and physics; some of us are parents, others nonparents; both married and single; and diverse social and political backgrounds—whatever area of expertise or perspective we need, we can usually find it among our members.

Besides critiquing our works, we support each other. We discuss our writing and publishing progress at the beginning and end of our meetings. We share experiences with publishers, editors, and agents, for the remainder of the group to learn from. If an author reports difficulties, we try to offer advice and possible options. We exchange market information, professional opportunities, and information on events in the field. A publication event is always celebrated. Further, we uplift each other in events outside our writing lives: medical crises and personal challenges find us ready to help.

Another distinguishing characteristic of our group is that we have also worked as a writing team. One day, one of the members of our group suggested that we write a novel together. Each of us had a novel in progress at that time, but none of these novels had been published. The proposal was that, by working together, we could come up with a terrific group novel and the resulting publicity might draw attention to our individual novels. Some members thought that project sounded fun and joined in for the challenge. Not all of the Aaardvark members elected to work on the project, so we all continued our usual activities at regular Aaardvark meetings. Those of us working on the novel (later titled *Autumn World*) met at separate, additional meetings.

First, we made a plan, including what sort of novel we would write, where the novel would be set, and who the characters would be. Having settled on a science fiction novel, we described the setting in detail (what sort of planet, how many moons, and so forth). Then we handed out writing assignments;

each of the project members wrote a certain number of chapters and took a viewpoint character. Once we had the initial chapters, we read those and decided how the story would progress from there. Subsequent chapters built on what had happened in the earlier chapters. Eventually, the novel was complete. To be sure of continuity, we met for a weekend at one of the members' houses, and read aloud the entire novel in sequence. That allowed us to eliminate inconsistencies and insert smooth transitions. As a result, the finished and polished manuscript became a very readable novel that was ready to send to publishers for consideration.

Our initial contacts with publishers met with repeated rejections. The two most common responses we received were that the novel was too short, or that the publishing house preferred not to publish a multiauthor novel unless one of the authors was already widely known. In fact, the multiauthor credit seemed to be a major stumbling block; experienced professionals told us that we would be better off submitting the novel under one pseudonym.

It took us nearly a decade of searching, but in the end, we did not find a publisher—a publisher found us. Members of our group talked about our novel at a science fiction convention panel discussion, and, unknown to us, a small-press publisher looking for material was in the audience. At the end of the day's activities, he e-mailed one of the members and asked to see the manuscript. Once again, a snag developed when we insisted that all five names appear on the front cover and title page, but when we convinced the publisher that this could be done without crowding the cover, the issue was amicably settled. After years of patience and persistence, *Autumn World* was published.

Our teamwork has continued through the publishing and publicity stages, in support of this title. Those Aaardvark group members who did not participate in the group novel enthusiastically supported the efforts of those who did.

When supporting this novel or a publication by one group member, we always speak about our group and the work of our members at conventions (as we did with our group novel). When one of us appears at a book signing or other public appearance, others of our group spread the word and attend the event. Those of us with Internet access post to newsgroups or e-mail lists. A couple of our members have even founded small presses, which has expanded group members' publication opportunities and allowed works to remain in print when they otherwise might have fallen out of circulation.

As a result, in the more than twenty years we've been together, the members of the Aaardvark have written and read a number of novels, short stories, articles, poems, songs, and Ph.D. dissertations—many of which have been published. Our members have won awards and critical praise. And, most important of all, we've had a grand time doing it . . . together.

> Find out what your hero or heroine wants, and when he or she wakes up in the morning, just follow him or her all day.
>
> —RAY BRADBURY

Dimming a Star

How to Manage a Dominant Group Member

DOROTHY STONE

~

WRITING GROUP NAME: Wayland Poetry Group
WRITING GROUP LOCATION: Concord, Massachusetts
TYPE OF WRITERS: Poets

A WRITING GROUP HAS a life of its own, a life that at times can seem to be directed by an assertive, strong-minded member. That is true of one group I am a part of, a disparate group with an interesting mix of backgrounds, life experiences, and styles. Our paths and obstacles along the way have all been different, so how is it that we end up in the same room, as if that had been the plan all along? Whatever the reason, we all admit that this room of shared secrets is exactly where we want to be. On one level we don't know each other well. Many of us do not see each other outside of this room, but we know whose son committed suicide and its impact on his mother who is still trying to forgive him. We share the depression years of a Massachusetts Irish family with too many children and too little money. We know whose mother and father have filled those roles lovingly and whose have failed. In poetic terms, we learn of divorces, deaths of loved ones, emotional deprivations, secret lives.

With such private material and the ways people deal with it under discussion, you'd think everyone would take a careful approach to the critiquing process. However, this is not always the case, which then leaves the group with a problem to resolve.

It's easy in a workshop situation for a strong individual to take on a leadership role before others realize what's happening. Before they know it, they may find themselves holding back, waiting for the star player to speak first, to pass judgment. After a poet has read his poem, before the majority has had time to absorb the whole and is still busy rereading the work before making comments or suggestions, the dissection begins. Some of these premature comments may come from an honest desire to share knowledge and experience, but if it gets too out of hand, there may be resentment or even a drop-off in membership.

Fortunately, there are ways to deal with or head off this problem. First, having a nonwriting group facilitator helps. It is her job to try to keep things on track and moving, to head off dominant takeover attempts. Since she does not have a stake in the offering of creative work, she isn't threatened or intimidated by anyone. If she sees a takeover happening or hears from members that they're feeling uncomfortable, she can speak in private to the outspoken person, showing how valued he is but asking him to pull back a little. Another step is to start one session with a discussion to redefine the aims of the group, to set some new ground rules for everyone to follow. In such discussions it's not necessary to single anyone out as an example; keep it general. If, after this, the behavior continues, the facilitator can tighten the leash a bit, controlling the meeting more than usual.

Not everything is the facilitator's responsibility, however. If you find the criticism somewhat off mark, don't be shy. Speak up. Challenge. Ask the others if they agree, and if they don't, encourage them to say what they think.

Another good way of breaking the habit of a solo member taking charge is to schedule a workshop session with an outside leader, a local professional who does not know the group or the habits that may be entrenched. Members will see another authority in charge, and it may change the dynamics of the group. This person, a local writer or teacher perhaps, could be paid by grant money or a group collection, or by some other means. It'll be money well spent, no matter how it's raised.

Another means of dealing with an outspoken writing group member is through humor. If, for instance, the star player's comments really have intrinsic value and he just needs reining in, as long as he has a sense of humor, warmly presenting a poem at one of the group sessions, such as the following one, might do the trick. Laughter clears the air, lightens tensions, erases anger. (A version of this poem appeared in the summer 2001 issue of *PIVOT*.)

> From two until four are precious sweet hours,
> for Allan dear Allan, is ours, is ours.
> His booming rich voice takes over the room
> and proclaims from on high our poetic doom:
> *"There is, however, just one change I'd suggest*
> *to put order and art into this tangled rat's nest*
> *of mixed metaphors and unpatterned rhyme*
> *and rhythm that dances to odd broken time.*
> *Begin at the end and cut all the rest.*
> *It's really two poems; the last line is best,*

and while you are at it, hyphenate here
and please spell correctly, my illiterate dear.
Self-expression ain't art, no matter how sad
your images are, quite simply, just bad.
But other than that a really good try.
Now let's move on; there're more fish to fry."
Yes, his wife may claim him for most of his hours,
but alternate Wednesdays, he's ours; he's ours.
We owe him a lot, oh yes we all do,
for we're better poets when he finally gets through.

In any group there will always be members who speak up more than others, whose instincts work rapidly, who do not mull over work as carefully as others. And there might well be members who shut out the whole poem while they focus on something that snagged their eye. There is, however, a time and a way to arrange for everyone to be equal, and that is through a public reading, given perhaps once a year. My group chooses April, National Poetry Month, for its annual presentation. Here everyone has a chance to shine. It's a fine way to work toward a common goal, to share a spotlight, to applaud each other's work, and to know we have dealt with life, our passion for writing, and each other.

Favorite Resources

BOOKS

Behn, Robin, and Chase Twichell, editors. *The Practice of Poetry: Writing Exercises from Poets Who Teach.* New York: HarperPerennial, 1998.

Strand, Mark, and Eavan Boland. *The Making of a Poem: A Norton Anthology of Poetic Forms*. New York: W.W. Norton & Company, 2000.

FAVORITE WRITING EXERCISE

This exercise, used in a small group under the direction of poet/facilitator Debra Kang Dean, could be used just as successfully in a larger group.

First, each participant submits three or four quotations, epigrams, or interesting facts on slips of paper. These can be compiled and handed out ahead of time for people to think about. Go to a museum or art gallery. Each person draws one or two of these slips of paper from a hat. Set aside a solid block of time to spend there—say, three hours. Split up and browse, linger where you wish, leave yourself open to what you see, keeping in mind the quote or quotes that you've selected. Find a corner and write something—a rough draft of a poem, the beginnings of one, whatever you feel like writing. It could even be a journal entry that you can go back to later and find usable ideas or images. After the allotted time, meet the other participants and, perhaps over coffee or a treat, read to each other what you've produced. Once you are at home, do whatever shaping and framing you want—from formal to free, from literal to metaphoric—and bring the result to a future group session, ready for critical feedback and, always, more work.

> **No tears in the writer, no tears in the reader. No surprise for the writer, no surprise for the reader.**
> —ROBERT FROST

Five Virtues That Toppled a Writing Group

ANN COOPER

~

WRITING GROUP NAME: Tuesday Writers
WRITING GROUP LOCATION: Boulder, Colorado
TYPE OF WRITERS: Mixed genre (poetry, short fiction, memoir, novels, children's, nonfiction)

I WROTE WITH the Tuesday Writers for eight years before the group drifted amicably from freewriting and critique to book appreciation, overcome by its own self-sabotaging virtues. We still meet regularly to discuss writing—our own and other people's—but our creative output has dwindled. I no longer turn to the group for inspiration or challenge. Since it is not uncommon for writing groups to fizzle, this cautionary tale is my attempt to pinpoint causes. Ironically, I believe we were brought down by former virtues: safety, friendship, longevity, comfort, and personal growth.

Safety

As a fledgling writer, I had plenty of ideas but lacked fluency and confidence. I needed a place to risk without ridicule. I was not ready for unkind—let alone savage—critiques. I'd met them in school and they left me shaking. I hoped a freewriting group would be safe.

Over the years, the Tuesday Writers sessions *were* safe. They let me follow wispy ideas to unexpected insights, try different genres and styles, and amass volumes of notebooks—compost files—to raid. I gained by listening to other people's raw writing and how they later developed it. I marveled at different *takes* we had on the same prompt. ("Where do we keep the _____?" unleashed a flood of excellent and varied stories that would not have shamed Dave Barry.) I learned that standard plots might be few, but ways to develop them are without number.

The more we got acquainted with each other through writing, critiques, and conversation, the more our sessions lost their edginess and unpredictability. We were like old married people who guessed thoughts before they were uttered. Critiques, which we conducted at one meeting in four, became *too* encouraging, to the extent that the committed writers in the group no longer took them seriously. The group had become utterly and claustrophobically safe.

Friendship

Our group, which spawned from a continuing-education writing class, varied from five (too small) to nine members. At the start, we were near-strangers. New people joined, stayed for months or years, and left. (One original member remains.) During the early years, a constant influx of diverse talent and viewpoints kept the atmosphere sparking and competitive enough to provoke experiment.

We had no formal leader. Our new-member accept/decline policy developed haphazardly, the criteria changing as we learned what mattered. In retrospect, we should have had clearly articulated procedures. We've had one man in the group. He lasted a few weeks before we (painfully) agreed to ask him not to come again. He wrote to impress, and his writing seemed contrived and dishonest. In the end, though, it was not his writing, but his taking ten minute timed writings so literally that he set his overly loud watch beeper, that finally convinced us that this male was another species.

Later, our informal rules that all writing should be considered fiction and no personal stories should be shared outside the group fell by the wayside. We knew so much about each other from writing and talking that we were *too* good friends. We began to procrastinate about bringing in new talent, each of us reluctant to be responsible for introducing a new member who might upset the existing balance. It became more important to preserve friendship than to maintain writing excellence. This undermined the vitality of the group.

Longevity

We aged together. Once, we represented a spectrum of outlooks, women from thirty-something to sixty-something, living different phases of our lives. We failed to replenish the group with youngish talent. As more members slipped into senior career responsibilities or, later, retirement, the collective writing energy waned.

Comfort

For many years, our group met on neutral territory—the university commons, our public library gallery or meeting room, or, in summer, outdoors (or on a Chautauqua porch once used by the Beat Poets). We met, wrote, and critiqued for an hour and a half, then left feeling energized and seething with literary good intentions. Later, because public space was hard to come by, we began meeting in members' homes. We met straight after the workday, so the comfort of someone's sitting room proved seductive, the facilities welcome. Socializing and eating escalated, as if each host felt obliged to shine. Warm and well fed, we got too comfortable. Writing and critiquing suffered.

Personal Growth

The current members all grew immensely through the group membership, but we grew in different directions. And of course, relative to our writing, we didn't all succeed equally, or at the same time, or up to our secret expectations. Whenever anyone achieved publication, we celebrated. But tension developed when one member declared she didn't want to hear about others' successes because they were too threatening.

In time, the group expanded to fill other needs: stress release after heavy days laden with job responsibilities, family therapy—freewriting as support prose. Some who imagined they wanted to write discovered they didn't want it enough, but they wanted to stay with the group because they valued the friendships so highly—not the original intent. We should have been clearer from the start that in a *writing group* individual friendships should be secondary to the writing.

~

I will always be grateful for the years when our group worked well. I'm proud to remember a fall retreat when we assembled and self-published a collection of Tuesday Writers' work. I lament the virtues that brought us down—too much ease, too little edginess and new blood, too much focus on friendship— at the same time as I thoroughly applaud these same virtues in everyday life.

What would it have taken for the Tuesday Writers to survive? We should have recruited actively, especially younger members. We should have insisted on a solid commitment to writing for continued membership. Above all, we should have risked more, challenged ourselves to rise above the familiar and comfortable, and been more prepared to shake up the group before rigor mortis set in.

Favorite Resources

BOOKS

Bernays, Anne, and Pamela Painter. *What If*. New York: HarperCollins, 1990.

Biffle, Christopher. *A Journey Through Your Childhood*. Los Angeles, CA: Jeremy P. Tarcher, Inc., 1989.

Goldberg, Natalie, and Judith Guest. *Writing Down the Bones: Freeing the Writer Within*. Boston, MA: Shambhala, 1986.

Smith, Michael C., and Suzanne Greenberg. *Everyday Creative Writing: Panning for Gold in the Kitchen Sink*. Chicago, IL: NTC Publishing Group, 1996.

FAVORITE WRITING EXERCISES

WRITING ESCAPE

An annual weekend getaway serves to refocus energy and set goals for the upcoming year. We relax after intense writing by switching media. The creative art projects—cut and paste, glitter, and fat crayons—free us up and bring forth insights, both on the page and in conversation, while we're busy being kindergartners.

Here are some examples.

■ **LIFELINE.** Select a dozen milestones in your life and illustrate them in any way you wish, such as using magazine cuttings, odd words, glitter, glue, and borders. One participant wrote "My Life in Chocolate," which later became a poem.

■ **WHO AM I?** Fold a long, five-inch wide strip of heavy paper back and forth to make a two-sided accordion book. Fill each page with words, photo clips, and ornamentation that conveys some aspect of yourself, your writing life, your frustrations, and your ambitions.

■ **MY WORDS.** Write down twenty or so snippets—quotes, thoughts about writing or about life—on different shapes, sizes, and colors of paper, and toss them in with everyone else's snippets. Choose several statements that appeal to you—for content, color, shape, or other criteria—and develop a narrative around them, adding your own comments and insights. For example, the phrase: "Writing is like _____" evolved into "Writing is like a food . . . sometimes sweet, sometimes bitter, sometimes nourishing, ofttimes junk," and "Writing is like a country . . . foreign, with no maps, and no return ticket to safety."

Dominating the Ugly Jade Dragon of Jealousy

CONNIE HECKERT

~

WRITING GROUP NAME: Bettendorf Public Library Juvenile Writers
TYPE OF WRITERS: Children's fiction, nonfiction, poetry, young adults

WRITING GROUP NAME: Quad Cities Branch of the National League of American Pen Women
TYPE OF WRITERS: Children's nonfiction, newspaper and magazine writing, romance, nonfiction, poetry, adult fiction, inspirational

WRITING GROUP NAME: Juvenile Forum
TYPE OF WRITERS: Writers for children; nonfiction, fiction, poetry

WRITING GROUPS LOCATION: Bettendorf, Iowa

"I LEFT THE Tuesday library meeting really bummed out," Anna said at our Wednesday evening critique at Butterworth Center. Anna and I are in two groups together; one focuses on writing for children and the other considers all genres.

"I mean," Anna continued, "I was really happy for everyone but I felt so depressed. Everyone had good news but me. Sara has a poem in an anthology and a new story in *Pockets* and the edited version of her picture book. You just sold a poem to *Highlights for Children* and a nonfiction feature in *Cricket Magazine*. A few weeks ago, my mother sold an easy reader to Grolier.

"And all I do is wait to hear back from editors," Anna continued. "When I picked up my son, he asked how my meeting was. I told him 'not so good—everyone had something new published but me.' He rolled his eyes, and said, 'But Mommy, you've had something published!'"

Anna is a warm, talented person who is new to writing and actively submitting work to publishers. The members of our critiquing group want her to succeed and we know she will, soon, because she's working hard on producing good work and writing fine cover letters. Her marketing efforts are well researched and she pays attention to where her work is and how long it's been there. And besides, our writing group helps her in every way we can.

Writing groups offer great support, but there are moments when the jade dragon of jealousy can rear its ugly head. At these times we may want to run away and hide in a cave where we can write in peace and not be confronted with competition and professional envy. Instead, it's better to dominate that dragon, and say to yourself, "my turn will come."

The value of writing groups far outweighs the occasional pangs of self-doubt and jealousy that erupt when colleagues share good news. Some of the most successful writers have experienced these feelings firsthand. Mem Fox, an Australian writer who has experienced considerable success with picture

books such as *Time for Bed* and *Tough Boris*, devotes an entire
chapter to writing groups in her adult book, *Dear Mem Fox, I
Have Read All Your Books, Even the Pathetic Ones*.

Fox was in a writing group where, although they had much
in common, she was probably the writer in the group who made
the ugly jade dragon rear its head for the others. Once she
started publishing in the United States, her books became
popular with children and adults. News of speaking engagements and author tours in the United States would make anyone jealous.

Over the years I've doggedly juggled my family's schedule
to attend writing meetings. As a writer, my soul requires the
sharing that comes from a common interest in literature and
producing something that contributes to our culture in a positive way. There are many more reasons why I am wholeheart-
edly committed to attending the three writing groups I support.
Here are just a few.

- These meetings give me concrete deadlines to complete a
  reasonably polished draft for readers. They also allow for
  socialization and a time for sharing current news, marketing tips, or publishing gossip—even if the sharing makes
  us jealous of someone else's achievements. Writing groups
  need material to discuss. It may be critiqued in hard copy
  prior to the meeting, brought to be read there, or simply
  read to the group for feedback.

- These gatherings are often more interesting when I have
  something on the table. Not having a manuscript in
  progress doesn't prevent me from attending, but to make
  the most of the meeting, I try to put work out there for
  feedback. Of course, there are times when I don't like the

comments, or I discount someone's opinion for one reason or another. But more often than not, I am invigorated when we discuss a piece I wrote. And I look forward to taking the most helpful advice from the drafts that are returned to me.

- In Ralph Keyes's book *The Courage to Write: How Writers Transcend Fear*, he addresses manuscript readers from family to friends and from poets to prose writers. "In the guise of 'seeking feedback,' many writers are trolling for compliments. When they ask for your opinion of their work, too often they mean your praise." Compliments and praise may make us feel good about ourselves, but usually these words don't go far enough in helping writers. This is why family members, unless they are highly qualified as literary critics, aren't the best people to ask to read and comment on your work.

- We become better writers and marketers, and gain more savvy in working with agents and editors in the field, if we constantly strive to grow. Consider your writing group as an ongoing class where homework is shared, and discussions occur that challenge and inspire you to broaden your knowledge. Invite people to your writing group who are at your same level or more advanced. Heidi Roemer, assistant regional advisor to the Illinois' Society of Children's Book Writers and Illustrators (SCBWI), recently said at a conference, "Every group can benefit from an advanced writer who is willing to share his or her experiences and expertise." The old adage that you won't be a better tennis player unless you play with someone who is better than you applies to writers, too.

- Book recommendations, magazine article endorsements, and the competitive urge that comes from listening to someone else's success stories motivate us to learn more about our own field of interest. One of the groups I meet with weekly gathers at the library where we often hand books across the table saying, "This is a great book. I haven't checked it in yet, but you can check it in and back out to read."

- Writing groups are kinder forms of writing workshops. In a very real sense, writing groups are made up of more tactful writers than those often found in workshops. Writing workshops, in my experience, are often larger groups of people who may be insensitive to the writer's feelings and tender ego. Truman Capote, author of *In Cold Blood*, advocated workshops and association with other writers as a positive force in a writing career. He said, "Any writer, and especially the talented writer, needs an audience. The more immediate that audience is the better for him because it stimulates him in his work; he gets a better view of himself and running criticism."

So when someone shares his or her success with you or members of your writing group, make an effort to celebrate the victory and enjoy the camaraderie and support of your critique group. It doesn't hurt to confess your feelings, as Anna did (at a time and place where the achievement wasn't dampened). But after acknowledging your feelings, slap that ugly jade dragon on its nose and say to yourself, and mean it, "My turn will come." Then remember all the wonderful gifts that come from being a part of your writing group, and go back to your manuscript and work it through again.

Favorite Resources

BOOKS

Fox, Mem. *Dear Mem Fox, I Have Read All Your Books, Even the Pathetic Ones.* San Diego, CA: A Harvest/HBJ Original, 1990, 1992.

Keyes, Ralph. *The Courage to Write: How Writers Transcend Fear.* New York: Henry Holt and Company, 1995.

Lamott, Anne. *Bird by Bird: Some Instructions on Writing and Life.* New York: Anchor Books, 1995.

Lerner, Betsy. *An Editor's Advice to Writers: The Forest for the Trees.* New York: Riverhead Books, 2000.

Marcus, Leonard. *Dear Genius.* HarperCollins, 1998.

Safire, William, and Leonard Safire, editors. *Good Advice on Writing: Great Quotations from Writers Past and Present on How to Write Well.* New York: Simon & Schuster, 1992.

Ueland, Brenda. *If You Want to Write: A Book About Art, Independence, and Spirit.* St. Paul, MN: Graywolf Press, 1987.

Zinsser, William. *On Writing Well.* Revised, fifth edition. New York: HarperCollins College Publishers, 1995.

RETREATS AND CONFERENCES

SOCIETY OF CHILDREN'S BOOK WRITERS AND ILLUSTRATORS (SBCWI)
Scbwi@scbwi.org
SBCWI has an annual conference in Los Angeles, midwinter conference in New York, and regional conferences in many states

and countries. (I sold my first national picture book to Clarion Books, New York, a Houghton Mifflin imprint, as a result of attending an SCBWI conference in Missouri.)

UNIVERSITY OF IOWA'S SUMMER WRITING FESTIVAL
100 Oakdale Campus W310, University of Iowa, Iowa City, IA 52242-5000
(319) 335-4160
Students participate in weeklong or weekend workshops in Iowa City, Iowa. All genres offered.

WEB SITES

www.bookweb.org
American Booksellers Association

www.ala.org
American Library Association

www.BookSense.com
BookSense

www.writers.net/agents.html
Internet Directory of Agents

www.nwu.org
National Writers Union

www.scbwi.org
Society of Children's Book Writers and Illustrators

FAVORITE WRITING EXERCISES

Write a short narrative about something you did in the last five years that shows a change in your character or personality. You may use compare and contrast between your life now and as it was five years ago, an anecdotal style, or dialogue. Or you may specify a particular incident that demonstrates a larger truth in your life.

Pretend you are an artist about to sketch. Go to one of your favorite places, a lake, a park, or a college campus teeming with life. Take notes and identify what you see, hear, feel, smell, and taste. Create a piece of writing that conveys this sense of place. Come to a conclusion about the scene and incorporate that into the piece you write inspired by this outing.

Art is a jealous mistress.
—RALPH WALDO EMERSON

The Awards of Writing

MARY-LANE KAMBERG

~

WRITING GROUP NAME: Kansas City Writers Group
WRITING GROUP LOCATION: Olathe, Kansas
TYPE OF WRITERS: Poetry, short fiction, essays, fiction, nonfiction, cookbooks, newspaper and magazine articles, science fiction, inspirational, children's, and young adult

THERE ARE MANY *rewards* to the writing life. But sometimes an *award* or two is in order. The writing group that I co-lead has been around since 1965. Here are a couple of reasons why we continue to survive and thrive.

The Amazing Grace Award

There's a golden statuette making the rounds in Hollywood, and it's not an Oscar.

But for those who receive it, it holds greater significance. It's a Mickey Mouse trophy that actors pass around to those among them who have accomplished something significant in their careers. Nicolas Cage has received it twice. And watching him talk about it during a televised interview some years ago, I thought what a wonderful idea it would be to have such a traveling award for our writing group.

And so the Kansas City Writers Group's Amazing Grace Award began. It's a golden statuette of *Victory*, a female angel (or is she a goddess?) with arms reaching to the sky and wings spread behind her. Her right hand holds a torch, and with her flowing skirt, long hair, and bare feet, she looks like Deborah Kerr in some strange movie. The inscription on the small walnut base says, "Kansas City Writers Group/Amazing Grace Award/Founded 1996.

The award goes to a group member who does something amazing. Other than that, no rules exist. Whoever currently holds the award passes it on within weeks, months, or even years of receiving it. The timing and criteria are solely up to the current holder based on whatever that person deems *amazing*.

To date, eight writers have received the award. Some receive it for reasons related to publication, but not all. The award has been presented for a writer's first sale, book publication, placing in a national poetry competition, and receiving honorable mention in the annual *Writer's Digest* Short Story Writing Competition. Others have received it for winning a censorship lawsuit against a local school district and for selling a short story to the *Kansas City Star* (which *never* runs fiction).

So far no one in our group has won an Oscar or become as famous as Nicolas Cage. But those who have held the Amazing Grace Award share the same kind of honor—the encouragement of friends.

Persistence in Writing Award

If a picture is worth 1,000 words, what are 100 rejections worth?

In the Kansas City Writers Group, they're worth a certificate signifying that the member has achieved official status as writer. The Persistence in Writing Award certificate, which is suitable for framing, advises the recipient to "Take heart, Noble Author, *Gone with the Wind* was rejected thirty-nine times."

The award began several years ago because so many of our members were reluctant to submit their work. By acknowledging the rejection aspect of a writing career, we wanted to recognize those among us who actively pursue the business end of the craft.

We address the business side at the beginning of our weekly sessions with market news. This is a time for announcements of new markets; new editors at old markets; and writers' conferences, readings, and book signings of interest to the group. Those who have published a story, poem, article, or book pass around the publication. We also announce the sale of work for future publication, signing with an agent, and getting rejections.

When someone announces a sale or brings in a published work, we applaud. And since we began the Persistence in Writing Award, the group applauds rejections, too, because a rejection slip signifies that the writer is marketing his or her work.

By offering these two awards, we accomplish several goals. First, we recognize outstanding achievements by our members. Second, we encourage members to submit their work. And third, we teach them to *laugh* at rejections instead of *crying* about them.

Favorite Resources

BOOKS

Bugeja, Michael J. *The Art and Craft of Poetry*. Cincinnati, OH: Writer's Digest Books, 2001.
This text offers instruction, examples, and exercises.

Drake, Barbara. *Writing Poetry*. New York: Harcourt Brace Jovanovich, 1993.
This book's easy to read and understand and features a lot of suggested exercises.

Goldberg, Natalie, and Judith Guest. *Writing Down the Bones: Freeing the Writer Within*. Boston, MA: Shambhala Publications, 1986.
Every writer should read this book.

Vogler, Christopher. *The Writer's Journey: Mythic Structure for Storytellers and Screenwriters*. Studio City, CA: Michael Wiese Productions, 1998.
Information: (818) 379-8799 or www.mwp.com.
Don't even think about writing a novel or screenplay until you have read this book.

Zinsser, William. *On Writing Well*. New York: Quill Harper Resource, 2001.
This is hands-down the best book on nonfiction writing technique, bar none. And it's fun to read. The techniques also apply to fiction and poetry.

CONFERENCES

Iowa Summer Writing Festival
University of Iowa, Iowa City, Iowa
www.uiowa.edu/~iswfest/
There are weeklong and weekend workshops throughout the summer.

Maple Woods Community College
Kansas City, Missouri

www.kcmetro.cc.mo.us/maplewoods/writeConf/2002%20site/
WC2002.html
This writing conference is held annually.

Maui Writers Conference
www.mauiwriters.com
Held Labor Day weekend this is the very best writing conference
in the whole wide world. There were more than 1,000 attendees last year. Here's a link to an article I wrote about it: www.
potpourri.org/editor/travel/travel_enchanted/travel_
enchanted.html.

**If you have someone on the set for the hair, why would
you not have someone for the words?**

—LOUIS MALLE, director, telling producers why he wanted
John Guare around during the filming of *Atlantic City*

PART IV

VENTURING BEYOND THE WRITING GROUP SETTING

■

> Writing ought either to be the manufacture of stories
> for which there is a market demand—a business as
> safe and commendable as making soap or breakfast
> foods—or it should be an art, which is always a search
> for something for which there is no market demand,
> something new and untried, where the values are intrin-
> sic and have nothing to do with standardized values.
> —WILLA CATHER

A day will come when you're ready to venture outside the safety of the writing group and share your work with the world. Whether it's sharing your writing by organizing public readings, shopping a book proposal, selling copies of your self-produced anthology, networking, or attending writing conferences, these essays will give you ideas on how to share your work beyond the group gracefully.

KaBooM!, The Kentucky Book Mafia

Secrets of Successful Marketeers

LYNN PRUETT

~

NAME OF WRITING GROUP: KaBooM!

WRITING GROUP LOCATION: Lexington, Kentucky

TYPE OF WRITERS: Fiction writers, poets, essayists, biographer, novelist, short story writer

IN JANUARY OF 2000, as the five members of our writing group sat around a kitchen table eating lentil soup, one member said she'd been to the local bookstore and hadn't been able to find Kentuckian Mary Ann Taylor Hall's story collection, *How She Knows What She Knows About Yoyos*. The member had prevailed upon the booksellers to move the book to a place of prominent display. We at the kitchen table laughed and said in jest, "We should do that for all Kentucky writers," and "We'd be the Kentucky Book Mafia!" and then, "KaBooM!"

The group had been meeting for two years or so at that point. We'd focused on becoming better writers but we hadn't thought, until we became KaBooM!, about the business part of a writing career. By midsummer we were learning how to write query letters in quest of literary agents. By the time September rolled around, we were on our way to New Orleans, 900 miles away, to attend the Words and Music Festival.

We had gone on writing retreats together as a group. Some of us had taken workshops at the University of Kentucky and at the Carnegie Center for Literacy, but we had never done anything as bold (or as expensive) as crossing five states to promote our writing. We selected Words and Music because writers are guaranteed manuscript consultations with editors and agents. Since literary agents weren't going door-to-door looking for writers in Kentucky, we understood we had to go to them.

Before we left for New Orleans we decided to treat this conference as a professional business venture. We had business cards made: they featured a gangster hat, the words *KaBooM!*, *The Kentucky Book Mafia*, and our individual names, street and e-mail addresses, and phone numbers. We gave these out to appropriate people, much to the delight of those who received them. We also decided ahead of time that we would take turns standing up in each session and asking an intelligent question. By the time the conference was over, our group was well-known to the writers, editors, and organizers of the event. I met Amy Williams, who became the agent for my novel, *Ruby River*, which she subsequently sold to Atlantic Monthly Press.

That experience cemented our focus. We could succeed in the literary world. We simply had to pursue avenues seriously. Professional development became our mission. After much debate over the financial and family strains such action would create, three members of the group applied for and were accepted into the MFA program at Spalding University in Louisville.

We continued to meet weekly at the Carnegie Center in Lexington to discuss work-in-progress, but we added a business portion to the workshop during which we shared writing opportunities and events. Currently we act as consultants to others interested in running successful writing groups. Last summer we launched a literary happy hour series, which features readings by KaBooM! while guests sample appetizers and beverages. (We hand-addressed postcards announcing the first event and ninety people came!)

The writing group has made a huge difference in my writing career. I wouldn't have considered going to New Orleans if the rest of them hadn't agreed to go. I would not have met Amy Williams in person and I would probably not be getting ready to go on my book tour. Others in the group, particularly the ones at Spalding, will attest to the difference our collective goals have made in their development as well.

I don't think any of us are natural self-marketers. But as a group, we have accepted the need to make our work public, and we have embarked on this path with a shared drive. It's exciting to go to workshops and receive the encouragement to push beyond safety zones, to apply for fellowships, send work out to publications, attend conferences, speak publicly as advisors, write reviews, give readings, and continue to improve our work. We honor our writing by shepherding it into the public sphere. Without this effort, we'd still be dreaming.

Favorite Resources

The following are books that inspire me and publications that include the work of one or more KaBooM! members, as well as my novel.

Behn, Robin, and Chase Twichell, editors. *The Practice of Poetry.* New York: HarperPerennial, 1992.

Brown, Susan Christerson. "Outside Looking In," *Journal of Family Life*, November, 1999.

Burroway, Janet. *Writing Fiction: A Guide to Narrative Craft*. Fourth edition. New York: HarperCollins, 1996.

Erdrich, Louise. *The Blue Jay's Dance*. New York: HarperCollins, 1995.

Oakes, Elizabeth and Jane Olmsted. *Telling Stories*. Bowling Green, KY: Western Kentucky University Press.
This collection includes "Porches" by Lynn Pruett, pp. 103–119; "The Red Cave" by Pam Sexton, pp. 149–169; and "Women's Secrets" by Crystal Wilkinson, pp. 247–255.

O'Connor, Flannery. *The Habit of Being*. Edited by Sally Fitzgerald. New York: Vintage Books, 1979.

Pruett, Lynn. *Ruby River*. New York: Atlantic Monthly Press, 2002.

Sexton, Pam. "Game Afoot," Henry Leadingham Prize in Poetry, folio. Monterey, KY: Larkspur Press, 2002.

Walker, Alice. *The Same River Twice*. New York: Scribner, 1996.

Wilkinson, Crystal. *Blackberries, Blackberries*. London, England: Toby Press, 2000.

———. *Water Street*. London, England: Toby Press, 2002.

Get Out of the House!

Master Public Readings with the Help of Your Writing Group

JENNIFER TAPPENDEN

~

WRITING GROUP NAME: DCW (only members know its meaning)
WRITING GROUP LOCATION: Kenmore, New York
TYPE OF WRITERS: Poets, essayists, and short story writers

THERE'S NO WAY AROUND IT, writing is a lonely art. The solitary creative process results in a manuscript that rarely receives face-to-face feedback from editors. All that rejection can leave a writer feeling isolated, and worse, irrelevant. A writing group can help alleviate some of those feelings, but even a great writing group can wind up in a rut. That's when it's time to get out of the house, and take your group along! Nothing creates a buzz like hearing and being heard!

Local literary events are a great place to start. Open mike nights, friendly to spoken-word artists, are a staple of both bookstores and coffee houses. Ask at your favorite establishment if they host literary events. Even if they don't, the staff will likely be able to suggest other places that do. Start paying attention to flyers in libraries and the listings of cultural events in your local newspaper. All it takes is a lead on one venue, and you'll be off and running. If your whole group is searching, it won't take long to compile a list of places to try.

Now comes the crucial part: actually go! Don't worry, no one will make you wear a beret or drink strange coffee (unless, of course, you want to). Make this first visit a scouting mission. Bring a friend or two from your group and plan just to listen. It's important to gauge a venue's personality, to ensure that it is compatible with your own. If you are a slam poet, you'll feel out of place at a venue leaning toward more formal material. This will help you select work to read there on future visits, and it also gives you a chance to pick up on etiquette. Especially important is keeping to the limits on the amount of time or the number of pieces each reader is allowed. Nothing shows more disrespect for an audience than monopolizing the microphone!

On your next visit, sign up to be a reader. Bring along your writing group for moral support. They'll be sure to clap for you, as well as to make sure you don't chicken out at the last moment. Better yet, encourage them to read as well. Mention your membership in the group whenever you read; if all your members do the same, you'll begin to cultivate a group reputation, as well as an individual one. It takes courage to read before an audience, but if you've done your scouting you already know that this venue is in tune with the type of material you write.

You'll also already know which of your poems would be best to read there. Prepare and order your material before you arrive to avoid fumbling at the podium. It is wise to leave your originals at home in case someone confuses your notebook with their own. This will also allow you the option to sign and give away a copy of your poem to anyone who might ask. Another useful tip: avoid reading from handwritten manuscripts. You wouldn't believe how many writers get to the podium only to discover they can't read their own writing! A clean copy in large type will prevent you from bending low over your work, and reading in a halting, tentative voice as you try to decipher your scribbles. You'll make a far better impression by standing straight, and looking up occasionally from your work. Follow along on the page with your fingers to avoid losing your place. And if you really want to wow an audience, memorize! (This might be something to work up to, and a word of caution: always have a copy of the piece available, as memory is often imperfect!)

Make notes on your manuscript to help you read more smoothly. Highlight words you wish to give extra emphasis. Practice reading your work aloud beforehand, and it won't just be your writing group out there applauding! If you are especially apprehensive, practice with your group as a test audience. Then on the night of the reading, you will be used to performing for them; their friendly faces in the audience will be a focal point for you, keeping your confidence from wavering.

Once the reading has ended, talk to the event's organizer and the other writers whose work you enjoyed. They are a wonderful source of feedback, both about your work and your reading style. They will also be good sources of information about other literary events where you and your group may share your work. If you are not currently a member of a group (or are not satisfied with your current group), this can be a good place to find out about other opportunities.

Eventually, by continuing to participate in open readings, you may be asked to anchor an event. This entails preparing a longer selection of your work, and usually your name is mentioned in any promotion. There may even be an honorarium.

Encourage the other members of your group to come and hear you, and if they are willing, to serve as readers themselves. Remember to introduce yourselves as members of the XYZ writing group! Supporting each other in this manner may then lead to an invitation for the entire group to be featured together.

Congratulations! You have transformed yourself and your group from writers to writer-performers! In time, both the group and its individual members will develop a following—rewarding in its own singular way—a public fellowship in addition to the more private one you share with your group.

Favorite Resources

BOOKS

Goldberg, Natalie. *Long Quiet Highway*. New York: Bantam Books, 1993.

Goldberg, Natalie, and Judith Guest. *Writing Down the Bones: Freeing the Writer Within*. Boston, MA: Shambhala Publications, Inc., 1986

Nelson, Victoria. *On Writer's Block: A New Approach to Creativity*. New York: Houghton Mifflin, 1993.

Strunk, William, Jr., and E. B. White. *The Elements of Style*. Fourth edition. New York: Longman, 2002.

ORGANIZATIONS

THE INTERNATIONAL WOMEN'S WRITING GUILD (IWWG)
Caller Box 810, Gracie Station, New York, NY 10028

www.IWWG.com

This organization's quarterly newsletter *Network* includes publication/contest opportunities. Programs include "Remember the Magic," an annual, weeklong writing retreat, the annual "Meet the Authors/Meet the Agents" event in New York City, and several other retreats throughout the year in various locations around the United States.

JUST BUFFALO LITERARY CENTER
2495 Main Street, Buffalo, NY 14214
www.justbuffalo.org
Local writing organization that runs seminars, readings, art-in-schools programs, and more.

THE UNIVERSITY AT BUFFALO POETICS PROGRAM AND ELECTRONIC POETRY CENTER
http://wings.buffalo.edu/epc/
Excellent poetics programs.

WRITERS & BOOKS
740 University Ave., Rochester, NY 14607
www.WAB.org
This organization is similar to just buffalo (listed above).

> **Only those who will risk going too far can possibly find out how far they can go.**
> —T.S. ELIOT

La Groupe or How I Learned to Get from the Stage to the Page

L. Claire Kincannon

~

WRITING GROUP NAME: OECD Writers' Workshop
WRITING GROUP LOCATION: Paris, France. Kincannon currently resides in Paeonian Springs, Virginia.
TYPE OF WRITERS: Poets, playwrights, screenwriters, short story writers, and nonfiction writers

"HELP! My husband brought me to Paris a year ago last week. Now I can't talk, tell time, or get a legal job!" And so I wrote. I wrote to exorcize my frustrations, my humiliation, my being treated as ignorant . . . as a child. Surprisingly, I found truth in all of the above plus gobs of tongue-in-cheek humor when I stopped to analyze all the funny incidents that occurred each day I walked out the door of our lovely Paris apartment, or even dared to pick up the telephone. But, to test how funny the words were on the page, I needed a listener. My spouse wasn't interested. Besides, he was too close to the story as one of the main characters and would challenge my words. So I found a group. We were associated with an international organization, the Organization for Economic Cooperation and Development (OECD), mostly through our spouses. We were all from different backgrounds, different religions, different home countries. Some did not have the command of English as a mother tongue. The only thing we shared was the fact we were all women living in Paris, France—not our hometown. Certainly the humor would be lost. Wouldn't it? Would they laugh *with* me? At my American sensibilities to all things foreign?

Our first meeting began in grand style at the home of the Japanese ambassador to the OECD. Present were Christina from Germany; June from Australia, but born in Poland; our hostess, Yuri, a Japanese diplomat's wife; Henrietta, born in Brazil of British and Dutch heritage; and me, the only American . . . or, I should say, the only one from the United States of America since I learned to be sensitive about such sweeping claims. Over the next two years, our group gained Margaret from Scotland, noted for her bagpipe prowess as well as her poetry; Iris, another Scotswoman by way of Canada; and Jitka, a doctor and wife of the ambassador from the Czech Republic. Last to join our group was the Irish octogenarian Kathleen, who came to Paris to study in 1945, married a Frenchman, and never looked back. Quite a stellar group, wouldn't you say? I was awed by the company and exceedingly shy about reading my chapters aloud as I had planned.

We met at a different home every other week for the next year. This proved to be both a blessing—the food and surroundings, mostly plush, were tended by servants—and a curse, since the atmosphere was formal and strained. Eventually, I supplied copies of the pages I wrote to all at the meetings. And, I read aloud before they gave comments. Not many laughed, but they were not shy about giving serious constructive criticism.

Their comments were accepted or rejected, but they were always fascinating and revealing of cultural differences. No one else wanted to read aloud. They simply handed out sheets of poetry or prose for us to read silently and then critique. So it was surprising that at the end of that first year we decided to give a performance night. June, the Australian from Poland, had much experience reading her dark, brooding poetry around the various Paris venues, and she convinced us we should try. "It doesn't resonate unless you read aloud," she admonished.

Our performance was titled, *Sheets to the Wind*, a title with a number of connotations from the literal to the obscure. My apartment provided the dramatic space to perform with its winding staircase and balcony overlooking the audience of maximum capacity (thirty-five) and a view of the Eiffel Tower from the terrace. We designed invitations and programs in the form of a collage on a scroll (Japanese influence). Although no theme was predetermined, what evolved was a generational tracing of the women in our families going back, for some, as far as five generations. Our writing, be it poetry or prose, reflected those women who influenced our lives—knowingly or not. We gathered pictures of great-great grandmothers and daughters, granddaughters, and so on, and blew them up, creating enormous collages as a backdrop for each participant. It was astonishing to see the physical characteristics thread their way through the generations.

Yuri, Kathleen, Henrietta, June, and I nervously prepared for the big event by rehearsing and critiquing our work simultaneously. We used a bedsheet as a device to weave through the performance from one reader to the next, connecting the varying vignettes. First as a shroud, a swaddling cloth, a bridal veil, a bedsheet, then a sailing sheet to the wind as it mingled with sheets of writing paper and fluttered from the balcony to the floor below.

We all learned a lot that night. Audience reaction had never been part of the equation before. Hearing the words, rather than just seeing them on the page, be they poetry or prose, exposed another dimension. The most astonishing discovery for me was to see how these five diverse women from five very different cultures had more similarities than differences. And we were all intricately connected.

∼

The group continued into a second year with renewed anticipation. We met in a small office conference room at OECD headquarters. The atmosphere was decidedly more serious and the food was nonexistent. At year's end no one wanted to do a performance night again. "Why not a book?" someone suggested. My American (USA) bravado jumped on that idea. I could contribute a chapter from my book about Paris, which was nearing completion. That would provide the incentive for someone to publish it. And besides I had experience as a graphic designer and cared about how the book would look so I volunteered my services. And we could have readings at all the big Paris bookstores. My American (USA) entrepreneurial spirit was threatening to the others. "Let's just staple some pages together," offered Canadian-Scotch Iris. But I convinced them we needed to think big! All we had to find was a little seed money to help defray the printing costs. We did, and we found a reasonably priced printer, too. We also found additional contributors who would pay a small fee to be part of our book in exchange for free copies of the finished product. We also planned a big kick-off celebration, which in hindsight we shouldn't have done until we had the books in hand (printing delays). Then we started compiling and editing all the material. Little did I realize then what a monumental task was before us, one that ultimately became mine to carry to fruition.

Four months . . . four excruciatingly painful months later, *Sheets to the Wind* was introduced to the world at a major Paris bookstore, covers barely dry. Included within its beautiful purple and lipstick-red cover were the words and images of nineteen women (including all of the original five) from eleven different countries. Twelve of the women featured in the book read that evening and on many Paris evenings thereafter. It was a triumphant debut.

One year later, I introduced my own book, *Paeonian to Paris*. There was laughter and a sense of accomplishment as I watched people react to my work. "The book looks good and feels good in my hands," and, "I haven't laughed so much in I don't know how long" were samples of high praise uttered at the end of my reading.

Now, two years later, and back in the United States of America, my publishing company, Dancing Ink Press, is about to publish *Sheets for Men Only* (an anthology of male writers) and a bilingual cookbook, *Vive la Soupe!* A reissue of *Sheets to the Wind* with a CD recording of the women contributors' voices is in the works along with my sequel, *Paris to Paeonian with Fresh Eyes*, which details, in a funny way I hope, my re-entry into this country after eight glorious years in Paris.

So . . . *Bravo* OECD Writing Group! *Bravo Paris!* I'm indebted to your inspiration. *Mais oui!*

Favorite Resources

BOOKS

Holt, Robert Lawrence. *How to Publish, Promote, and Sell Your Own Books*. New York: St. Martin's Press, 1986.

Kincannon, L. Claire. *Paeonian to Paris*. Paris, France: Dancing Ink Press, 2000.
A humorous American perspective of day-to-day life in Paris.

———. *Sheets for Men Only: An International Anthology of Male Poets and Writers*. Paeonian Springs, VA: Dancing Ink Press, 2002.

———. *Sheets to the Wind: International Anthology of Women Poets & Writers*. Paris, France: Dancing Ink Press, 1998.

Lambert, Martine, and L. Claire Kincannon, editors. *Vive la Soupe!: Bi-lingual (French–English) Soup Cookbook from Friends and the Famous*. Paeonian Springs, VA: Dancing Ink Press, 2003.

> **The writer is by nature a dreamer—a conscious dreamer.**
> **—CARSON MCCULLERS**

Getting Feral Parakeets to Go on Paper

Adventures in Publishing an Anthology

R. Neube

~

WRITING GROUP NAME: Cincinnati Writers Project
WRITING GROUP LOCATION: Cincinnati, Ohio
TYPE OF WRITERS: Two fiction, one nonfiction, and one poetry critique group; Neube's fiction critique group is open to writers at all skill levels and includes novelists, and mystery, western, science fiction, romance, and short story writers

D<small>URING THE DECADE</small> the Cincinnati Writers Project's (CWP) fiction critique group has been meeting, we often talked about publishing a collection of our members' stories. The ultimate weakness of gathering twenty-five writers in a single room was our penchant for prattling through every conceivable detail for countless hours. If all that jaw-energy and hot air could be harnessed, we could have provided electricity for a small town . . . like Tokyo.

We discussed producing a modest chapbook with a few stories and poems. After inspecting the cheesy look of even the best chapbook, our enthusiasm quieted, despite the economy such books offered. Indeed, the marvels of desktop publishing promised we could run off copies on our own computers. That simply seemed too much like asking a parent to be our prom date.

We discussed a newsprint format to give us room for a dozen stories. Here entered the economy of scale. By producing a few thousand copies, we could get the unit cost down to a dime. But how could we finance those thousands? Selling ads to cover the expense would allow us to distribute the papers for free, a price we were confident the public would accept. Alas, between the alternative presses, the special-interest and rant tabloids, the advertising budget for most area businesses was already committed.

At every turn, problems rose like mountains. Whereupon, we discussed them for hours and hours, making the mountains all the taller.

Barb Lukas, a veteran member of our critique group, took this publication idea as her personal mission. Her optimism saw no problems; her boundless joy for the written word gave her the energy to tackle the naysayers. She collected cost projections and started planning to scale the mountain. Alas, she died unexpectedly, which killed the project.

Years ticked away. Sometimes the topic would be resurrected on the lips of a newcomer. Other times, our old-timers would recall Barb's mission with a broken heart. We spit-balled possibilities for hours and hours.

Enter print-on-demand (POD) technology. A cyber-savvy member mentioned visiting a Web site that offered to publish professional-quality tradeback books for no more than the cost of the volumes themselves. The potential excited our group into a frenzy of yet more discussion.

Everyone was willing to volunteer someone else to do the work. Acrimony erupted as folks debated how we might select stories for the anthology. A jury? A lottery? A three-tiered elimination? Novice writers feared the published members would dominate; new members fretted the veterans would restrict the collection to old-timers.

All this grief before we started.

Time ticked. Every week, somebody would mention the project to me. "Great idea, unless this person or that gets involved."

Rob, our cyber-guy, found a plethora of firms in the POD business, all promising this was the future of publishing. A sage consumer, he checked out reputations, checked the experiences of ex-customers, and kicked those cyber-tires. He even discovered a Web site where users rated POD publishers (www.aspiringauthor.freeuk.com/podsurvey.htm).

Once again, discussion bloomed at group. What size would the stories be? Would we have a theme? Who would judge the stories? More hours wasted on trivial details when the big question—who has the time to do this?—remained unanswered.

Simple question, simple answer. *Nobody* had the time.

But the memory of Barb nagged at me. I had always felt guilty that I hadn't supported my dear friend more when she first espoused the project. So I decided to *make* the time for the anthology.

At our next meeting, Rob delivered the news that the free publishing offers were history. While our jaws flapped, the POD business had moved on. Now the publisher we had our eye on charged a hundred dollars for their low-end package, and three hundred for a deluxe package, which offered perks, including the option to furnish our own cover art, rather than use their stock covers, as well as promotional opportunities.

Knowing our group could spend months debating the ground rules—and who knew how much the POD industry would be charging by then?—I embraced my inner Mussolini. Getting together with Rob, we forged ground rules. I would handle the editing side, dealing with the writers and CWP board of directors; Rob would handle the cyber side, dealing with the publisher.

We walked into the next meeting, distributed a sheet of rules, and requested a yes/no vote on the project. No debate allowed. The vote was unanimous.

Our first and foremost mission was making certain our authors would get paid for their work. This would not be a vanity effort. For maximum fairness, my partner and I decided that any story submitted before our deadline was guaranteed inclusion in the anthology. The tales were to be e-mailed to me as an attachment. That would be the last the author saw of the story until the anthology was published.

At every corner, Rob and I streamlined the process. We believed from womb to tomb the project would take ninety days.

I am told that in the right light you can read the word *moron* in the furrows on my forehead.

Thanks to an enlightened board of directors, the CWP gladly financed the three hundred bucks we needed to get started. When I showed them how many copies our prospective authors wanted, the board also agreed to finance the purchase of the volumes themselves—the bulk of the project's cost. That relieved me of the prospect of collecting sales money up front like a maniacal Girl Scout on a cookie binge.

Stories began to arrive—*.doc, *.wps, *.things I'd never seen before. I opened the files with my Microsoft Word 97, playing word processing roulette. Some opened perfectly; others opened with freaky symbols all over the text, as if an alien had intercepted the file and critiqued it in Betelgeusian.

I spent days removing the alien symbols, catching a few missing commas, perchance a misspelled word, and polishing the occasional clunky sentence. Once I had finished the stories on hand, I opened the documents again to give them one last inspection. Much to my horror, the alien material had returned and my edits had vanished. A week's work had been wasted. What was I doing wrong? Blundering through the mess until I found a solution by trial and error cost me more days of work.

After the project was over, my computer guru would say, "Your people should have sent their stories in *.rtf format. No mess. No fuss."

Of course, no sooner had I finished curry-combing the stories than authors began to send me new versions, breaking the rules. "This one is better," they would say. How could I argue with that?

Two of our contributors wanted to run their stories through our critique group before submitting them. How could I argue with that?

In the end, we collected eighteen stories. Only two months behind schedule, only two hundred hours of my life invested, I handed the anthology to my partner who formatted it in accordance with POD guidelines, then submitted it electronically.

Whereupon we learned that when the publisher said a stage took a week, it took a fortnight. Ten days equaled a month. When they said their software could handle any cover we sent, they meant any cover *except* the one we sent. More weeks vanished.

Upon receiving the proofs, I was chagrined to find typos I had missed. Correcting those cost us extra. Speaking of cost, I had neglected to include paying our artist for the cover in our initial budget. The CWP board was understanding when I asked for more funds.

Overbudget and behind schedule, we finally took delivery of *Feral Parakeets and Other Stories*, two hundred and forty pages of sweat and glory. I heard Barb's spirit chuckle when I glimpsed a writer aglow at the sight of her first story in print.

What did I learn?

- Publishing a collection of your group's stories will take longer than you think.

- It will cost more than you think.

- Be a smart consumer. Check out your publisher before spending a penny.

- If you are a computer dolt like me, team with a cyber-savvy person. And don't be too proud to ask questions when those documents arrive with weird symbols.

- Demand all your stories in *.rtf format.

- Have as many contributors as you can get. Their friends and relatives will buy copies.

- Don't discuss it.

- Do it!

Favorite Resources

BOOK

Spinrad, Norman. *Staying Alive: A Writer's Guide*. Virginia Beach, VA: Donning Company, 1983.

CONVENTION

www.contextcon.com
Context
This is my favorite science fiction writing convention.

WEB SITES

www.cincinnatiwriters.com
Cincinnati Writers Project

www.sfwa.org/members/neube

> **Writing is the hardest way of earning a living with the possible exception of wrestling alligators.**
> —WILLIAM SAROYAN

Encouraging Our Parakeets to Leave the Nest

Helping Our Anthology Find New Homes

R. NEUBE

~

WRITING GROUP NAME: Cincinnati Writers Project
WRITING GROUP LOCATION: Cincinnati, Ohio
TYPE OF WRITERS: Two fiction, one nonfiction, and one poetry critique group; Neube's fiction critique group is open to writers at all skill levels and includes novelists, and mystery, western, science fiction, romance, and short story writers

I HAD 150 COPIES of *Feral Parakeets and Other Stories* stacked in my living room. The fiction critique group's anthology owed our parent organization, the Cincinnati Writers Project (CWP), $1,574—largely the cost of the volumes. A CWP board meeting loomed within a fortnight, and I hoped to return that money to the treasury by then as my personal apology for being overbudget and four months behind schedule. My goal could be accomplished by selling 105 copies. The remaining forty-five were pure profit. Our eighteen authors could split the pot of gold and buy their loved ones a Big Mac. Who knew, the sky was the limit, maybe they could even super-size their fries.

Our critique group met every Wednesday, so mere days after their arrival, my partner, Rob, and I unveiled the paperback. Between authors and members wanting to support their peers, we sold seventy-four copies that night. I was dancing in the street.

But I had exhausted my marketing ideas after futilely trying to turn our authors into salespeople. (Can't get writers to do anything useful. They are as bad as my cats.) Having spent so much time and energy in the editing phase, I gave insufficient thought to selling our opus.

President Amy of the CWP and Cathy, vice president of promotions, came to the rescue of *Feral Parakeets*. After Rob found a bar willing to lend us their second floor for an evening, Amy and Cathy organized and publicized a launch party. Several of our authors read their stories to the public, some experiencing that nerve-racking exercise for the first time. They ate, drank, and raised the roof. We moved another twenty-five copies.

We were inches from profit territory when the sales began to stall.

In my original computations I failed to take into account promotional copies. The owner of the bar who hosted our launch party deserved a freebie, didn't he? We sent copies to newspapers who never reviewed us. The Ohioana Library Association requested two free copies in order to review them for their members. How could we refuse them? An on-line bookstore asked for a freebie to read in order to decide whether they would purchase copies. Never heard from the company again. Those volumes did not wreck our income flow, but . . .

We then encountered a big surprise.

There was a dirty little secret about print-on-demand (POD) books that the publisher failed to mention on its Web site. POD firms offered no returns, no juicy price cuts, no incentive whatsoever for a bookstore to stock them. Chain bookstores forged corporate policies *not* to buy them; many of the struggling independent booksellers could not afford to stock them.

Thanks to a personal contact of President Amy, we scored an anthology reading at a major chain that shall go unnamed because I hope someday they will stock my novels. Sure, they allowed us to read our stories—they supported local writers. They even deigned to let us distribute fliers about how to order *Feral Parakeets*. We just couldn't sell copies on the premises. We did have a writer with a criminal bent who stood outside the store with copies hidden under her coat. "Hey, mister, want to buy some hot fiction?" Alas, she only sold a single copy.

In Cincinnati, we are blessed with Don Hild, owner of the small but influential Mount Adams Bookstore, a true believer in local writers. He provided us with space for a Saturday morning reading and bought seven copies as well.

Don's example inspired us to approach other independents in our area. OK, we were buying at $7.50 and retailing at fifteen bucks. Most stores expected a 60/40 cut, which meant they wanted to buy our anthology for nine dollars, a profit ouch, but doable. I launched a series of phone calls and e-mails; I even dropped into bookstores to talk with overworked managers. They saw so many self-published people, only the smoothest survived. If only I was friction-free.

The CWP Web site offered us a platform to tout our work among our membership, as well as curious Internet visitors. I volunteered the use of my post office box for mail orders. Rather than take a copy to my friendly postmaster to learn how much mailing them would cost, I guessed the postage. As a result, I ate eighty-seven cents every time I mailed an anthology as penitence for my blunder. Only a handful of orders arrived by mail.

Meanwhile, our publisher's Web site was hard at work touting our effort. Their promises had led me to believe they would host a dazzling *Feral Parakeet* Web page designed to seduce the buying public into ordering millions of copies. Instead, our anthology merited a site that inspired my twelve-year-old nephew to offer his help designing a better Web page.

Our publisher sent notices to hundreds of bookbuyers. Alas, when *Feral Parakeet*'s birth announcement came bundled with offers for *A History of Lint in Romania*, potential buyers trashed it all as junk mail. Little wonder our first royalty check from sales on their end came to $4.50.

Every week an e-mail alert from our publisher told us how they could print copies to stock book shows and library conventions, even provide our soldiers overseas with our anthology. All we had to do was send them money, money, money. It became pretty obvious how the company made its bucks.

Then there was the issue of apathy. We had published our milestone . . . and nobody cared. Much to my surprise, the apathy legions included several of our authors.

As luck would have it, one of our critique group members freelanced for the major alternative newspaper in the tristate area. Kate worked overtime on her editor asking to write an article about *Feral Parakeets*. Instead, her editor proved more interested in our use of POD technology. Ah well, any publicity was better than none, and a really cool picture of Rob appeared with the article.

Our team worked the neighborhood newspapers after the *Cincinnati Enquirer* made it clear that sewer taxes interested them more. In the tristate area, there were fourteen such papers.

One took our bait, profiling the author whose story titled the anthology. The other thirteen yawns deafened us.

I once talked to a hostess of a cable access talk show bemoaning the dearth of participants for her program. I contacted her. "Writers write," she said. "People don't care unless they're famous. Besides, your writers look like...writers." At least she replied, which is more than I can say about the other cable access shows I contacted.

On the bright side, despite my ineptitude and the general chaos, those 150 volumes had finally gone out my door. A glutton for punishment, I used our profits to order another hundred copies.

Our authors are going to have to wait for their royalty checks, but I think we're catching on to the rules of the game.

What did I learn?

- Print-on-demand technology may not be ready for prime time, but it offers your writing group a chance to publish its own work.

- Nobody else cares. Cope with it. You're going to have to care enough for everyone.

- Get as much help as you can during the promotion phase.

- Try every bookstore, newspaper, and cable show, however large or small. At least one of them will want to help.

- Don't rely on the phone and e-mail. Face-to-face selling still works best.

- Keep plugging. The only way you lose is when you quit.

Moving Beyond the Meetings

Having Fun and Adding Quality with Group Events

D. M. ROSNER

~

WRITING GROUP NAME: The 6' Ferret Writers' Group
WRITING GROUP LOCATION: Fairfield County, Connecticut
TYPE OF WRITERS: Fiction writers, primarily novelists

IN 1992, after meeting every other week for three years, The 6' Ferret Writers' Group came to a serious decision—it was time for a Halloween party. While it might sound like nothing more than a fun evening, that party had an enormous impact on the long-term success of our group. It was the first of many events that stretched us as writers and expanded our ideas of what a group was all about.

The Halloween party concept began during a meeting, when we thought it would be fun to write Halloween stories. We had plenty of experience doing writing exercises. In fact our name came from a circle story. (That particular story, written a line at a time by each member, continued to pass from person to person long after it had ceased making sense. The cry to kill it was answered with, "Just then, a giant 6' ferret driving an eighteen-wheeler came along and ran them all over. The end.") A Halloween writing exercise, it seemed, would be easy.

We all went home to write, but at the next meeting we discovered that none of us had a solid idea for a plot, and the party was only two weeks away. We discussed our story fragments, hammered out a common theme, and each wrote the same story from a different point of view. On the night of the party, dressed as our characters, we read the stories aloud, and had a good laugh. The party became an annual tradition, and each year we print up a small anthology of the stories for our members.

Over the years, the Halloween concept evolved, and now we often choose an overall theme for the stories—past themes have included New Orleans, the New Millennium, and even Star Trek. We also draw ideas out of a hat. These ideas are usually broken down by category, such as Odd Object, Animal, Character, Supernatural Element, and Food (the chosen foods are brought to the party, which has made for some interesting meals). Some of the stories have been serious, some funny, but we always have a great time with them. We've also learned to avoid vampires as main characters in our stories—if you're wondering why, try reading twelve pages aloud while wearing vampire teeth.

Don't think that an annual party has no real value, though—what started out as a simple extension of the group has resulted in the publication of four of our Halloween stories. Not bad for a writing exercise.

~

Once we discovered that a group could be more than the sum of its meetings, we began looking for other ways to expand our activities. The next idea we had was something we call Novels

Days. A Novels Day is simply a Saturday or Sunday set aside to work on our current projects. There is no set schedule of meeting dates—we simply hold them whenever we feel the need. We meet somewhere for breakfast, and chat about what we hope to accomplish for the day or any blocks we're having, then adjourn to a member's home to write. It is not a time for discussion, although we do run the occasional question by one another. We continue writing until we run out of stamina, which is often around midafternoon.

After a few years, we found that a day simply wasn't enough—and thus we departed for our first annual retreat. We booked rooms off-season at a seaside motel, and devoted three days to our work. That weekend gave us a basic blueprint for our retreats, and each year we refined it until we found the atmosphere and routine we needed.

Our retreats go something like this: Get up, discuss work in progress or read the results of writing exercises over breakfast, then write. Break for lunch. Write. Break for dinner, then write or do writing exercises late into the night. Sleep, rinse, and repeat.

We prefer bed-and-breakfast inns because their rich atmospheres are perfectly suited to writing. In the past, we've moved from state to state for retreats, but in recent years we've settled on a wonderful Connecticut inn. Staying in the same place is not only more convenient for us, but our breakfast discussions— often about such things as disposing of bodies—frighten fewer innkeepers this way.

~

The addition of writing time isn't the only way we've moved beyond meetings. Most of our members are now published authors, and as a result we've had the opportunity to do book readings.

Our first member to have a story published in an anthology brought the book, copies of the advertising slicks, and a brief biography to her local bookstore, and asked if they'd like her to do a reading. They agreed. It was really that simple. Bookstores like to have authors do readings because it draws customers—so don't be afraid to approach them!

Opportunities for speaking engagements are all around, too. We have spoken at local bookstores about how to build a writing group, and were pleased with the enthusiastic attendance. An added benefit came when two audience members later joined our group.

If your group has an area of expertise—perhaps a particular genre or favorite subject matter—take advantage of the opportunity to share your knowledge.

So speak out. Do a reading. Throw a party. Stretch yourselves. Take your group to the next level, and move beyond the meetings. The results just might surprise you.

Favorite Resources

BOOKS

Bradbury, Ray. *Zen in the Art of Writing*. New York: Bantam Doubleday Dell Publishing Group, 1992.

Goldberg, Natalie. *Thunder and Lightning: Cracking Open the Writer's Craft*. New York: Bantam Books Inc., 2001.

Lamott, Anne. *Bird by Bird: Some Instructions on Writing and Life*. New York: Anchor Books, 1995.

The 6' Ferret Writers' Group. *Don't Forget to Write! A Guide to Building and Maintaining a Lasting Writers' Group.* Philadelphia, PA: Xlibris, 2000.

Zinsser, William. *On Writing Well.* New York: HarperTrade, 1998.

WEB SITES

www.6ftferrets.com
This is the official Web site of the 6' Ferret Writers' Group.

> **Writing is about getting something down, not about thinking something up.**
> —JULIA CAMERON

Networking and the Writing Group

David Starkey

~

WRITING GROUP NAME: Untitled
WRITING GROUP LOCATION: Santa Barbara, California
TYPE OF WRITERS: Poets

SOMETIMES WRITERS come together simply for fellowship and encouragement. Many groups start like this—and many remain this way to the end. Clearly there's nothing wrong with camaraderie among like-minded individuals. However, writing groups can also offer ambitious writers the opportunity to bring their work to a much larger community.

Aspirations for greater things may in fact be already present in a group, even if no one has articulated them. Group members may worry that if they talk about networking too openly, they'll appear pushy, careerist, unspiritual. The group may well have formed simply because a few people wanted to share their joy in putting words to paper, to write, like Keats, "for the mere yearning and fondness . . . for the Beautiful even if the night's labours should be burnt every morning and no eye ever shine upon them." Yet nearly all writers are, if not openly, at least secretly, ambitious. Keats certainly was—and readers centuries later are glad of the fact. To recognize and harness this ambition for the benefit of all members is truly a service to the group.

Consequently, groups thinking of turning outward to the larger world would do well to heed the following suggestions.

1. **Make networking a part of every meeting.** Though they will obviously vary depending on the members, every group has certain core expectations. Perhaps one expectation is that members show up on time, or that everyone takes turns hosting a meeting, or that members always bring sufficient copies of their work. Whatever the expectations may be, they are established early on and are part of the identity of the group.

   It's not, therefore, unreasonable to add one more expectation: that networking be a legitimate part of every meeting. Some groups will find it easiest to incorporate the networking portion at the beginning, when everyone is settling in. Others will use it as a way to break the meeting at the halfway point. And others will wait until the end, when group members want to know how the praise they just received can translate into more tangible rewards. The significant thing is that there is a time set aside *every meeting*, that networking becomes as routine as saying hello.

2. **Invite each other to join as featured readers.** Public readings give a writer visibility in the community. Readings offer writers rare opportunities for face-to-face interaction with their audience. They provide much needed ego gratification. They challenge the shy and reward the outgoing. More often than not, they are a great deal of fun.

Readings also provide group members with an opportunity to help promote each other's work. This is best accomplished when a group member is either the featured reader or part of a large collection of readers. In the former situation, the group member may well have the power to say, "I have a friend whose work is terrific. I think the audience would really enjoy her. Can you open up a fifteen-minute slot so she can read?" And when a group member is part of a sizable assembly where everyone reads for, say, five or ten minutes, it usually doesn't take much effort to have one more person added to the ensemble.

3. **Share tips on places to publish.** In many respects, publication is the most lasting and most concrete form of public approbation for a writer's work. In any thriving writing group, some or all of the members are actively seeking publication. Sharing tips on new markets is beneficial on several levels. First, it's impossible for every writer to know every market, so information about new markets keeps everyone in the group up-to-date on new trends and new places.

   Often a member will receive a rejection letter or a sample copy of a magazine that clearly indicates that the venue is not right for his or her work, but is ideally suited to someone else in the group. Once this sharing of information becomes routine, all group members will feel obliged to do their part. What goes around will come around in the form of more marketing opportunities for everyone's writing.

4. **Be humble about your own work.** For a writing group to function harmoniously, all members must, at some level,

feel they are equals—if not in outward achievement, then at least in potential. To realize this goal, it is the responsibility of the star (or stars) of every group to remain modest about their accomplishments. If a more celebrated member is in a position to network more frequently on behalf of other group members, she must remember that—should her efforts pay off—her fellow members will one day be able to work just as vigorously on her behalf.

5. **Collaborate on projects.** Collaboration is a part of any group. The simple fact of deciding when and where to meet requires a collaborative effort on the part of busy people. Discussing writers' drafts in the meeting involves a complicated process of consensus, adjustment, and partnership.

   Collaboration need not stop at this level. Writing together is an obvious next step: writing in response to each other's work, coauthoring poems, stories, and essays, interviewing each other and publishing the results. Coediting a print or on-line journal enables group members to become acquainted with and publish writers who may in turn be able to do a favor for one or more members of the group. The group that finds its way to publishing a book, perhaps as sponsor of a contest, becomes even more influential.

   In short, the more group members see their own interests as intertwined and mutually beneficial, the stronger the group will become.

6. **Establish expectations that group members will publish and read outside of the group.** Networking is obviously useless if it's all talk and no action. The implicit message of these suggestions is that group members should expect

each other to participate in the literary world outside the group itself. The writer who feels that simply because he is the star of the writing group he is also a de facto star in the larger community of writers is suffering from a delusion. It is a harsh awakening when that writer is inevitably exposed to others who have no stake in maintaining his ego. Hiding one's head in the sand of the writing group also diminishes one's desire to take risks, while networking encourages a writer to grow, to achieve beyond the safety of known boundaries.

Favorite Resources

BOOKS

O'Reilley, Mary Rose. *Radical Presence*. Portsmouth, NH: Boynton/Cook, 1998.

Rothenber, Jerome, editor. *Technicians of the Sacred*. Second revised edition. Berkeley, CA: University of California Press, 1995.

MAGAZINE

Poets & Writers
Also available on the Web at www.pw.org.

WEB SITES

www.clmp.org
This is a Web site for the Council of Literary Magazines and Presses.

http://eserver.org
This is a Web site where writers, artists, editors, and scholars
gather to publish and discuss their works.

http://groups.yahoo.com/group/conpo
Yahoo! Groups: Conpo—Literary Magazines and Literary
Contests

http://mockingbird.Creighton.edu/NCW/
This is the Web site for Nebraska Center for Writers.

> **Most writers regard truth as their most valuable pos-**
> **session, and therefore are most economical in its use.**
> —MARK TWAIN

RESOURCES

■

21 Tips That Put My Playwriting Group on the Map

LISA ROSENTHAL

~

WRITING GROUP NAME: The Playwrights Collective
WRITING GROUP LOCATION: Chicago, Illinois
TYPE OF WRITERS: Playwrights, screenwriters, novelists, and memoirists

SINCE MY PLAYWRITING group began in 1996 we've learned a few things. The following is a list of 21 of the most important—some came the hard way. The Playwrights Collective (TPC) continues to grow, evolve, and succeed as I write. And through it all I've always known there's no place I'd rather be developing my voice than among my TPC comrades.

1. **Your first date is an important one.** Once you've collected some people interested in starting a group, make the most of your first meeting. Collectively decide how often to meet, where, when, and at what time. Decide on the format (one member presenting his or her work each night or splitting nights among two or more members, read work at the meeting or beforehand but be flexible). Any fees to cover costs? Now

get those calendars out and commit to dates! In my group we set the schedule about three times a year so that we can book each member for one date each time.

2. **Meet regularly.** Our group originally met once a month and it didn't foster cohesion and it took forever to get a turn. Try to meet twice monthly at a minimum.

> **People think playwriting is just somebody supplying the words. No. Theater is the place where you learn all your lessons in a crowd. Imagine a novelist watching five hundred people simultaneously reading a draft of a novel and then making adjustments based on their immediate responses.**
>
> —JOHN GUARE, playwright, author of *Six Degrees of Separation*

3. **Remind members of the next upcoming meeting.** In our group whoever is presenting their work sends out a reminder e-mail. A presenter will often ask for RSVPs so he or she can plan how many scripts to have on hand and precast characters.

4. **E-mail is your friend.** Just think about the time it would take to contact ten people by phone to remind them of the next meeting (even if you leave a voice-mail message), and then think about how long it takes to send an e-mail message to several people simultaneously. 'Nuf said.

5. **Cover your ass.** OK, it's your turn and you don't have anything to present. Offer up your date and find someone else to fill it. At the very least keep in touch with all group members

to keep them informed of a change. Again, do this by e-mail. (Imagine how many phone calls *this* would entail.) If no one is prepared, suggest a group meeting topic (see Tip 18 below).

6. **Don't cancel!** Even if the person presenting doesn't have anything to present and no one else does either, meet anyway. Use the meeting to do writing exercises or make it a craft workshop. Everyone can share lessons they've learned about their writing or the business of writing. A key to maintaining a strong writing group is regularity. Keep the relationship going.

7. **If it's a collective, make it so.** Share the responsibilities needed to maintain the group. There's a contact sheet to maintain (with names, addresses, phone numbers, e-mail addresses, and maybe even directions to the members' homes), a schedule to set, and other issues to discuss, such as event planning. Since everyone benefits from the group experience, everyone can contribute to the maintenance of the group. If you set this up when the group is just forming, there should be few problems.

8. **Never forget the food.** OK, this is optional. But in my writing group, whoever presents their work also provides snacks. It can be as simple as a bag of chips and a bowl of popcorn or as elaborate as paté, Brie, French bread, and Merlot. (In my group the quality of the food is directly related to the nervousness of the presenter.) You can always assign someone else to bring the food but that's a whole other layer of organizing and remembering. If you prefer not to have the food interfere with your reading and critique, save it for dessert.

9. **Be prompt.**

10. **Take time to be friends.** Our group originally met at 7:30 P.M. but people wanted to catch up with each other so we

didn't get down to work until after 8 P.M. We now meet at 7 P.M. for chatting and get down to work by 7:30 P.M.

11. **Have expenses—have a fund.** My writing group started with a five-dollar-a-year membership fee to cover coffee and tea expenses. And there was money for postage if something needed to be mailed. If you're planning an event—such as a reading series or festival of new work—you'll need to collect more money from members to cover the additional expenses of printing, postage, whatever (unless you get a grant or find a patron). It may be easier to build up a larger fund if you ask for small monthly contributions. Remember, we're writers, not Rockefellers.

12. **Never apologize for the quality of your work.** Your writing group is absolutely a no-excuses zone. You are all there to learn, not to judge each other.

13. **Let the writer choose the postreading critique focus.** Is there a particular issue or question the writer has been trying to resolve? Getting the focus from the writer will help to ensure the most helpful comments for the writer. It will also eliminate the chance of a writer getting overwhelmed. If a writer is open to any kind of feedback, he or she will let the group know.

14. **Positive before negative.** Always start by telling a writer what you liked about his or her work. Then don't be negative, be constructive.

> **Life beats down and crushes the soul and art reminds you that you have one.**
> —STELLA ADLER

15. **Own your words.** Include phrases like "I think" or "I don't understand" in your critiquing comments. It's your opinion—own it with pride.

16. **Don't rewrite someone else's work.** Everyone has a unique way of exploring a scene, a poem, or a children's story. Offering help is different than rewriting a writer's work by telling them what they should have done.

17. **Don't be a diva.** A writing group is a collective community. It doesn't exist to serve the needs of any one member over any other member. Equitably share the time within each meeting. Don't be afraid to tell a member when he or she is monopolizing the feedback session.

18. **Feed the artist within you and build up the foundation of your group.** Being a writer is not just writing. It means reading books, going to stage performances or films, attending seminars or classes, observing life, and *living*! Plan group activities that are related to your craft so that you can share this as a collective experience.

19. **Plan shared presentation nights.** Critique each other's synopses, share upcoming contest deadlines and information, discuss iambic pentameter, compare notes on how to attract a film distributor—whatever.

20. **Celebrate change.** People's writing interests change over time and members of your group will meet with different levels of success. Accept this. Are you willing to critique other types of writing? If you want to maintain a member whose interests are expanding, this is a must. Celebrate everyone's achievements—what is good for one artist is good for *all* artists.

21. **Write!**

Favorite Resources

BOOKS

Lamott, Anne. *Bird by Bird: Some Instructions on Writing and Life*. New York: Anchor Books, 1995.

Rosenthal, Lisa. *A Dog's Best Friend: An Activity Book for Kids and Their Dogs*. Chicago: Chicago Review Press, 1999.
Come on, I have to plug my own book. After all, I wrote it to support my playwriting habit!

Singer, Dana. *The Stage Writer's Handbook: A Complete Business Guide for Playwrights, Composers, Lyricists, and Librettists*. New York: Theatre Communications Group, Inc., 1996.
This is an invaluable resource by the former legal counsel of The Dramatist's Guild of America.

Sova, Kathy; Samantha Rachel Healey; and Jennifer Sokolov, editors. *The Dramatist's Sourcebook*. New York: Theatre Communications Group, Inc., annual
This vital reference is published annually in August or September. It lists theaters, retreats, contests, fellowships, and more. It also includes details on each and great indexes to search by areas of interest or title, and a submission calendar to help you get organized so you don't miss any important deadlines.

Sweet, Jeffrey. *The Dramatist's Toolkit: The Craft of the Working Playwright*. Sixth edition. Portsmouth, NH: Heinemann, 2000.
Sweet has also written *Something Wonderful Right Away: An Oral History of The Second City and The Compass Players* (1987), *Solving Your Script* (2001), and numerous stage plays.

Wagner, Jane. *The Search for Signs of Intelligent Life in the Universe.* New York: Harper & Row, 1986.
This is the text of the show that was so brilliantly performed onstage by Lily Tomlin in 1985 and reprised from November 11, 2000, to January 21, 2001. A great example that less is more!

And any play you can get your hands on! You can learn from *every* play you read. Even if you don't like it, even if you think it's poorly written, and especially if you inhale it!

BOOKSTORES

ACT I BOOKSTORE
2221 N. Lincoln Avenue
Chicago, IL 60614
(773) 348-6757
(800) 557-5297
info@act1bookstore.com
www.act1bookstore.com
You don't have to live in Chicago to get their help—they mail.

THE DRAMA BOOK SHOP
250 W. 49th Street
New York, NY 10018
(212) 944-0595

> **I regard the theater as the greatest of all art forms, the most immediate way in which a human being can share with another the sense of what it is to be a human being.**
> **—THORNTON WILDER**

Fax: (212) 730-8739

info@dramabookshop.com

www.dramabookshop.com

WEB SITES

www.nycplaywrights.org
New York City Playwrights is not only an open writing group for playwrights, but its Web site also posts writing contests and calls for scripts from schools and theaters.

www.stageplays.com/markets.htm
The Playwright's Notice Board is updated regularly with contests and calls for scripts from theater companies around the world (but primarily the United States and England). This site also sells plays and gives playwrights an opportunity to list their work.

~

And finally, go to live theater! Storefront theaters, midsize companies, and Broadway touring companies—see it all! It's a great way to learn your craft and sustain the art you love!

21 More Tips to Creating and Sustaining a Successful Writing Group

1. **Take classes and attend seminars.** This is also a great way to recruit others to form your own writing group. Getting a taste of other writers' work and personalities in these settings will help you find a good fit.

2. **Don't be too hasty in forming your group.** Talk together, read each other's writing, and get familiar with each other's feedback style before declaring yourself a group. Commit to a couple of sessions and then review the dynamics of the group.

3. **Be clear about the group's goals.** Is manuscript feedback your focus, or are people looking to do writing exercises together, or to be led by a facilitator?

4. **Meet some place you feel comfortable.**

5. **Separate yourself from the work.** Other group members are critiquing your work, not you.

6. **Honor every writer's unique voice.** Help others clarify their intent to communicate it effectively to readers, not change the message.

7. **Honor everyone's vision.** What you find compelling helps define your uniqueness as a writer. Respect what other writers find compelling.

8. **Treat feedback like a gift from your mother-in-law:** If you like it, use it with pride; if you don't, quietly toss it aside after she's gone.

9. **Avoid distractions.** If you listen to music, listen to songs without lyrics so this won't compete with the dialogue in your head or distract you from reading and/or reflecting on another's work.

10. **Stretch, flex, shake out any tension in your body.** Leave your life and responsibilities behind. You are here to create art.

11. **Warm up with a writing exercise.**

12. **Be a teacher.** Share your writing, your experiences, and your knowledge with others.

13. **Be a student.** Be open to learn from others.

14. **Don't compare yourself or your writing to others.** We each travel a unique journey in our writing lives. Honor this.

15. **Put your work in front of an audience.** Hearing your work out loud and noting the reactions of audience members (sitting in the back is ideal for this) can help you further develop your work.

16. **Include the name of your writing group in your biographical material.** If all group members do this, the name and reputation of your group will grow.

17. **Promote the work of other writers in your writing group.** What's good for one is good for all.

18. **Share contest information with others in your writing group.**

19. **Seek out conferences and attend them as a group.** Separate and attend as many programs as you can. Then share what you learned with other group members as soon as possible while the information is still fresh.

20. **Go to artist retreats as a group.** Nothing beats getting away from it all to get it all together in your writing. Even a hotel room can be an artist's retreat. Novelist Maya Angelou and playwrights Terrance McNally and Wendy Wasserstein are just a few writers who write in hotel rooms. You can do this as a group, too. Where else can you get away from your bills *and* get room service?

21. **Delight in your accomplishments—big or small.** Share a personalized response from an editor with your group, teach everyone a terrific way you've found to organize your submissions or files, and celebrate dedication to rewriting by encouraging every effort.

It's much more important to write than to be written about.
—GABRIEL GARCIA MARQUEZ

10 Tips to Taking Your Work Public

1. **Create a Web site for your writing group.** Feature members' work and contact information. Update it regularly.

2. **Cross-pollinate with other writing groups and gain exposure for all.** Organize a reading or festival together. You can share the planning and expenses. You can also do this with artists in other disciplines such as musicians and visual artists.

3. **Offer freebies.** Charge an entrance fee to cover your expenses but also give attendees something to walk away with after the show, such as a collection of work read at the event or a bookmark with your group's Web site address.

4. **Host an out-of-town writer.** This may be an interesting enough angle to get media coverage for your writing group's event.

5. **Define your audience and then reach them.** Green-haired-tattooed-and-body-pierced teens your target audience? Post notices in the coffeehouses where they hang out or on school campuses.

6. **Encourage word-of-mouth at your event.** If people like your children's book or novel, encourage them to tell their friends, family, even strangers. This is one of the best (and cheapest) ways to spread the word.

7. **Be the squeaky wheel.** Get what you need by communicating your needs (without whining) to the media, your audience, or neighborhood bookstore. If you don't let others know what you need, how can they offer help?

8. **Have a mailing list sheet at every event to grow and keep your audience.**

9. **Involve volunteers in your event.** Appeal to people in your nonwriting life for help with ideas, mailings, whatever. Some people do not want to write but like to be a part of a creative community whether it's passing out handbills, greeting people at the door of an event, or helping out with a newsletter. Let others help you celebrate your work.

10. **Join a professional craft organization.** For example, The Dramatists Guild offers sample contracts and will review those you get from theaters that want to produce your work. The Society of Children's Book Writers and Illustrators (SCBWI) has a very useful Web site to find out about events in your area, meet other writers and illustrators with similar interests, and much more.

> **The artists who want to be writers, read the reviews; the artists who want to write, don't.**
> —WILLIAM FAULKNER

30 Tips to Marketing Your Work

1. **Seek out resource guides for your genre.** Many list contact information so you can find out the name of the person to whom you should address your correspondence, and much more. Before soliciting a publication, check the company Web site for changes in personnel, genres of interest, and location.

2. **Don't blindly send out your work.** Read several issues of a magazine, request a catalog from a publisher, see several films by a production company, or attend a few plays by a theater company before sending a query.

3. **Browse the Web for outlets for your work.** Create a list of key words and use a powerful search engine to mine for gold.

4. **Use concise query letters (no more than five sentences) for your initial contact.** *Don't* send your query via e-mail unless you are specifically invited to do so.

5. **Be confident.** Tell the theater professional/book editor/film producer why your play/book/screenplay is right for them. Don't be cocky, and don't be coy.

6. **Proofread your letter.**

7. **Never apologize for the quality of your work.** If you're that unsure of the material you're sending out, perhaps it's not ready to meet the public.

8. **Presentation counts.** Your materials should be neatly typed and presented.

9. **Do provide postage for a response whether it's a postcard or an SASE.**

10. **Use the correct amount of postage when mailing your materials.** Don't let them arrive postage due.

11. **Code everything!** Imagine this scenario: You sent a query a year ago and someone requests a copy of your manuscript or screenplay. Congratulations! Except you can't read the handwriting on the card and the postal station stamp is illegible. Who's asking for your work? If you place a small code on every SASP and SASE you'll know who's asking.

12. **Solicit outlets the way they want.** If they say to send a book proposal, three poems, or a ten-page dialogue sample, don't send them any more or any less.

13. **Enter writing contests.** Winning awards will open new doors for your work. Don't enter writing contests that require large entry fees for a small return. These are more fundraising efforts than anything.

14. **Be patient.** Responses take time. Many resource guides list the average response time.

15. **Fish regularly.** Send out queries constantly so you'll always have correspondence coming in and it will get your mind off how *l-o-n-g* you've been waiting to hear back from others.

16. **Keep track of your submissions.** Include contact information, what you sent, dates, and outcomes. This will free your mind so you have more creative writing time. It'll also guide you about when to follow up on submissions.

17. **Update your resume regularly.**

18. **Embrace those submission responses.** *Don't* call them rejections. Chances are it's a timing issue or your work isn't right for that publisher, theater, or producer. Let these responses remind you of all the hard work you've completed. Even a handwritten note on a form letter is a gift.

19. **Be courteous.** If someone does something nice for you or your work, let him or her know it.

20. **Build an e-mail or mailing list from your contacts.** Make it easy for people to keep track of you and your work. Occasionally mail updates about yourself and your writing accomplishments.

21. **Be your own PR representative**. Provide story angles for newspaper X about why your event Y is newsworthy. What makes it unique and special? Help members of the media figure this out by providing the who, what, when, where, and why of your event. These are the basic elements of a professional press release.

22. **Attend events where you can meet new people in your genre.** Networking can help create new opportunities and expose you to new ideas. It's important to support other artists.

23. **Pat yourself on the back regularly.** Acknowledge your hard work, improvement, and follow-through.

24. **Never devote all your time to marketing.** Give yourself time to write, rest, and enjoy your life.

25. **Share your marketing experiences with your writing group.**

26. **Value your experiences.** Even a negative experience can become a positive if you learn from it.

27. **Set deadlines for yourself.** Whether it's committing to a night on your writing group's schedule or managing your marketing correspondence, deadlines will help keep you on track with your writing commitments.

28. **Know that few artists can survive by their art alone.** Even Tennessee Williams worked twelve-hour days as a door-to-door salesman early in his writing career.

29. **It's all about balance.**

30. **Always make time for writing.**

> Art is a moral passion married to entertainment. Moral passion without entertainment is propaganda, and entertainment without moral passion is television.
> —RITA MAE BROWN

INDEXES

■

Index by Type of Writing Group

FACILITATED WRITING GROUPS

FANTASY WRITERS

FICTION WRITERS

IN PERSON

Index by Key Word

An Invitation to Writing Group Members

If you are a member of a writing group and would like to be considered as a contributor to future editions of *The Writing Group Book*, please send your name, address, telephone number, and a brief description of your group (no more than 250 words, please) to:

Editor, *The Writing Group Book*
Chicago Review Press
814 N. Franklin Street
Chicago, IL 60610

or

WGB@ipgbook.com